Navigating Leadership

Navigating Leadership

Tools for Leading Effective Organizations

Ruth Y. Cox
Esther C. Swink

www.navigatingleadershipbook.com

"This book will be a marvelous resource for enlightened leaders for many years to come. It is more than an affirming good read, it is really useful for important leadership dimensions — guiding both personal and organizational direction setting and providing a multitude of activities and tools for navigating there. It thoughtfully links and then builds on the best of past research and then clarifies and integrates the best of the emerging studies. I especially appreciated the timely and practical discussions of authenticity and the integrity of mind, body, heart, and spirit...really the heart of transformation."

DR. RICHARD BENJAMIN
Retired Superintendent of Schools
Senior Consultant for ArtsNow

"Using a nautical analogy, the authors have turned the search light on the secrets to leadership success in any field endeavor. Each section of this terrific book contains navigational tools to assist any organization in developing leaders to make a difference. I highly recommend this book."

DR. STAN TOLER
Bestselling Author & Speaker

"Esther Swink and Ruth Cox deliver a toolbox of resources that every leader will use again and again. Over several decades in every level of educational leadership from local schools to the university, Drs. Swink and Cox have gathered and organized the best tools and activities leaders use to strengthen work teams and advance their organizations. The six values out lined in the book are core issues for leadership, the instructions are clear and easy to follow, and the resources and activities are immediately applicable and effective. When consulting leaders or teaching a course, I use the information and exercises in Navigating Leadership."

DR. RICHARD LESLIE PARROTT
Professor of Education,
Founder/President of Seize Your Life, Inc.; Author

"For new leaders, a great set of tools to get started. For seasoned leaders, a wonderful set of reminders, to sharpen your leadership skills."

DON TWINING
Vice President Business Development
American Health Facilities Development

"The authors write from the real workplace of organizational experiences. Their references and resources are regarded among the best. The book is designed for greater development of an individual/group. The content focuses on doable — interactive — creative how to's — authentic — engaging of the group. The call to balance — not sameness — is worth the book."

DR. NINA G. GUNTER
General Superintendent Emerita,
Church of the Nazarene; International Speaker

"Thanks for sharing the copy of Navigating Leadership. I just finished reading it [*Navigating Leadership*]. It is the most 'tool rich' book for leaders that I've seen. I'm glad to endorse it."

DR. DAN BOONE
President, Trevecca Nazarene University

"If you're thinking about teaching an in-depth, top tier course on management — this is a book you must read and own. The authors have done the work for you. Or if you want to become a 'true north', truly qualified leader or manager — this is a book you must read and own. The authors have provided the information and the map for your success. My personal bookshelves are lined with books on management. But none of them is constructed like this one. It's a "must read" and a valued resource that's one of a kind."

DR. JIM VAN HOOK
Retired founder/CEO Provident Music Group,
CEO Word Entertainment, Dean Mike Curb College of
Entertainment and Music Business at Belmont University

"Leaders and those aspiring for leadership positions will find the book Navigating Leadership: Tools for Leading Effective Organizations a must-read. Effective leadership today requires trusting environments, empowering others and maintaining passion to reach one's goals. *Navigating Leadership* provides specific steps to develop these traits and much more!!"

DR. THERESE WILLIAMS
Director of Schools,
Catholic Diocese of Nashville

DEDICATION

....

To our Husbands, David and Jeff
    for their undying patience and support

ACKNOWLEDGEMENTS

....

The authors are indebted to:

Trevecca Nazarene University —
    for granting sabbatical allowing time to write

Members of the Cohorts in the Ed.D. program —
    for submitting ideas and encouraging us to publish

Students over the years —
    for providing a willing, albeit captive, audience

Graphic designer, Bill Kersey —
    for excellent work and wise counsel

Our Heavenly Father —
    for blessing us with opportunities to express creativity
    and leadership

Amen and amen.

TABLE OF CONTENTS

· ·

NAVIGATING LEADERSHIP: TOOLS FOR LEADING EFFECTIVE ORGANIZATIONS

Many organizations are like ships lost at sea, floundering in the waves and high winds of today's challenges. Organizations find themselves
- without effective leadership

- without trust,

- without direction,

- with subordinates without power,

- with different departments operating independently, and

- without clear goals and plans.

Not only in crises but in day-to-day operation, these obstacles keep organizations from fulfilling their purposes to the degree possible. In this compilation, an analogy of the ship as the organization is used to formulate concrete images. Just as ships need the lighthouse as a tool to safely direct them away from perilous conditions, so organizations need tools for safe navigation.

Lighthouses are constructed of different materials at different locations to serve different purposes based on the need of the area. Very few light-houses are the same but serve a particular area in specific circumstances. Just as captains of ships need navigational tools that are specific to their ships, in this compilation, there are different tools that you can use as an organizational leader in your quest to build unique, effective organizations.

This book resulted from numerous requests from organizational leaders. It differs from other books on leadership by providing practical "navigational tools" or "beacons" – namely, activities and resources that have been used effectively to improve organizations. These activities have been gathered from the personal experiences of the authors and from students in their doctoral studies.

In the six sections of this compilation, the following essentials include:
Examining Leadership
Charting Direction
Creating Authenticity
Delegating to Strengths

Aligning Operations
Starting the Journey

The organization of each chapter is as follows:
- One essential skillset is considered.

- A 'big question' lays the foundation for ideas presented.

- Using the ship as an analogy for the organization, a comparison is included.

- Tools are provided from which leaders may select to assist in developing that skillset.

- References to writings by recognized leaders serve as "anchors" to support the authors' ideas regarding each skillset.

Preparing to be an effective organizational leader is challenging and exciting work. The goal of the authors is that the tools in this compilation will result in helping you and your organization toward accomplishment of each skillset. We are pleased you have decided to join us on the journey.

Ruth Y. Cox
Esther C. Swink

Examining Leadership

WHY SHOULD YOU BE THE LEADER?

Just as a captain needs the compass to chart the ship's direction and to keep the ship on course, the captain must also use an inner compass to assure personal and professional effectiveness in the leadership role.

Regardless of where it is placed, a compass always aligns to true north. It is constantly and consistently attracted to the north because the magnetized needle at its heart aligns with the earth's magnetic field. If a ship's captain chooses not to follow the compass, it will likely be a foolish decision with disastrous results, preventing the ship from achieving its mission. The wise captain welcomes guidance from the beacons of the lighthouse and other navigational markers, acknowledges the need for assistance from a competent and committed crew, and is continually in touch with his internal compass.

The two most important days in your life are the day you are born and the day you find out why.

~MARK TWAIN

A wise leader chooses to be guided by the internal compass. From it emanates a passion for the chosen journey. When vocation becomes avocation, the result is focused authenticity so that everything aligns with the person's core.

Adherence to one's internal compass compels a person to dig deeper, reflect more fully, participate with those of like-mind, and heed guiding principles. Bill George (2007) suggested that each person has an internal compass, an inherent attraction to that individual's true north, resulting in an authentic life well-lived. An added benefit is that adherence to "true north" brings a sense of joyful accomplishment.

. . . .

No one can arrive from being talented alone. God gives talent; work transfers talent into genius. ~ ANNA PAVLOVA, RUSSIAN BALLERINA

. . . .

The first step to leadership development is self-development. This means first deciding WHY you choose to be a leader. Everyone who desires to be in a leadership position needs to examine personal motives, abilities, talents, and strengths. In a translation of work by Lao-tzu (1985), Lao stated, "To know how other people behave takes intelligence, but to know myself takes wisdom. To manage other people's lives takes strength, but to manage my own life takes true power."

TOOLS FOR EXAMINING LEADERSHIP

SKILLSET	Examining Leadership		
TOOL	Ask, Learn, Follow-Up, Grow		
IMPACT	✓ Individual	✓ Team	Group
PURPOSE	To obtain feedback to improve self-awareness, modeling, and influencing direct reports		

DESCRIPTION

- The leader schedules a one-on-one meeting to dialogue with direct reports (monthly, quarterly). The leader must help the direct reports feel comfortable, especially if this is a new technique.

- The dialogue is based on six questions with follow-up statements.

- The leader begins first each time so that the direct report is not trying to guess what the leader wants.

- The six questions with follow up statements are:

  1. Where are we going?

     I'll tell you where I think we are going.

     You tell me where you think we are going.

  2. Where are you going?

     I'll tell you where I see you and your group going.

     You tell me where you and your group are going.

  3. What are you doing well?

     I'll give you my sense of what you are doing well.

     You give me your sense of what you are doing well.

  4. What suggestions for improvement do you have for yourself?

     I'll tell you the suggestions I have.

     You tell me what suggestions you have.

  5. How can I help?

     I'll add anything else I think I can do.

     You tell me what I can do to help and support you.

6. What suggestions do you have for me?

    I'll tell you what I think I need to do.

    You tell me what you think I need to do.

DEBRIEF
? Embedded in activity

MATERIALS
✓ None

ADAPTED FROM
Goldsmith, M. (1997). *Ask, Learn, Follow-Up, and Grow*. In F. Hesselbein (Ed). The Drucker Foundation: *The leader of the future* (pp. 227-237). San Francisco: Jossey-Bass.

Kouzes, J. & Posner, B. (2002). *The leadership challenge* (3rd ed.). San Francisco: Jossey-Bass.

....

Reflection is really a process that begins with looking back on a situation, pondering over it, learning from it and then using the new knowledge to help you in future similar situations. ~ JENNIFER MOON

....

SKILLSET	Examining Leadership		
TOOL	Board of Directors		
IMPACT	✓ Individual	✓ Team	Group
PURPOSE	To develop a Board of Directors to serve as accountability partners		

DESCRIPTION

- Explain that leaders need a group of trusted friends and colleagues to serve as accountability partners.

- Have participants use the chart provided to:

    1. Identify a group of eight individuals who will support you AND will be honest with you about the areas in which you need to improve.

    2. Complete the Board of Directors chart with the names of your personal board. Include each person's relationship to you and the area of strength in which you believe each participant can serve as a mentor to you.

    3. Optional: Once developed, contact each proposed board member to ask their participation. They will need to commit to:

        ∿ Attending a meeting with you and other board members at least once a year to review with you your goals, strengths, and areas needing improvement and to give you support and honest feedback about your progress.
        ∿ Check in with you individually at least once a quarter to discuss your progress.
        ∿ Be available for you to call when you have decisions to make or concerns in their area(s) of expertise.

DEBRIEF

? What are the areas that you find most important to address?

? What are the possibilities to actually gather the Board of Directors together?

? What do you anticipate your board members to focus on initially?

? How can you embrace the information that your board would offer?

MATERIALS
✓ Chart per participant

BOARD of DIRECTORS

NAME

SKILLSET	Examining Leadership		
TOOL	20/20 Vision		
IMPACT	Individual	✓ Team	✓ Group
PURPOSE	To impress the importance of identifying and building on the values/vision of the organization		

DESCRIPTION

Note: This activity will require an extended time period with more than one meeting.

- Divide into teams of 5–7.

- Distribute to each participant five colored, adhesive dots and ask them to hold them until later in the activity.

- Distribute a worksheet with four questions and ask the team members to consider the organization and to answer the questions together at their tables. The questions are:

  - ❧ Who is important and what matters most?
  - ❧ What is our purpose and what matters most?
  - ❧ How we will treat each other?
  - ❧ Where are we going and how will we get there?

- After teams have answered the questions, ask them to identify seven values that apply to our organization and to identify a reporter for their group.

- Have a reporter from each team share aloud the values identified by the team.

  - ❧ Assign two scribes at chart tablets to record the values identified by the teams.

- Ask the scribes to cull the list, combining those that are similar, until a final list is completed.

- Engage in a discussion of what the values mean and attempt consensus on the meanings, creating a mini-definition.

- Ask each participant to vote for five values by placing one of their dots by each value they choose. The five values receiving the most dots will comprise the possible values for final consideration for the organization.

- Give participants who feel strongly about a value an opportunity to express why or why not one of the values should or should not be included. Attempt consensus agreement on the five final values.

- Assign a writing team (possibly volunteers) to wordsmith the five values including the mini-definitions for consideration by the group at another meeting.

- Have the writing team share their work on the 5 values. (This should be at a follow-up meeting.)

- Engage participants in discussion about the wording of the values and make any edits for which there is consensus.

- Ask each participant to consider/compare their personal values with the organization's values. Are they in alignment? Are there conflicts?

- Distribute a pair of oversized plastic sunglasses (or a paper cut-out of an oversized pair of glasses), large enough to write on, to each participant. Have them write the five values of the organization on the left lens of the glasses and one way that they will contribute to achieving the vision of the organization on the right lens.

DEBRIEF

? How do the values identified represent the organization?

? When a client or visitor enters the organization, how will they see the values in action?

? If values are not readily visible, what can be done to make them visible and real?

MATERIALS

✓ A pair of plastic, oversized sunglasses for each participant (If not available, use paper cut-outs of oversized glasses)

✓ Make worksheet for each team

✓ Colored dots

✓ Chart tablets

✓ Markers

SKILLSET	Examining Leadership		
TOOL	Helping Others Find Their Voice		
IMPACT	✔ Individual	✔ Team	✔ Group
PURPOSE	To address personal development as the basis for empowering and motivating others		

DESCRIPTION

Note: Understand that motivating others to "find their voice," as Covey (2004) stated, begins with the leader. It is necessary to address the elements to becoming the best person possible to be able to help others around me. This includes: cultivating mental ability, being an empathetic listener, are staying physically and spiritually fit.

- Have participants review the chart associated with both Personal Development and Empowering and Motivating Others. Use chart provided.

- Ask the participants to assess their level of adherence to each of the elements.

- Explain that individuals must address PERSONAL DEVELOPMENT before helping others. Overarching all self-improvement is vision, purpose, and self-discipline. Setting the example for others is a major influence.

- Explain that EMPOWERING AND MOTIVATING OTHERS requires an attitude of putting service to others above self.

DEBRIEF

? Embedded in activity. Use this exercise to generate an environment of reflection.

MATERIALS

✔ Charts for each participant

PERSONAL DEVELOPMENT		
	At what level am I? 0 – not at all 1 – somewhat 2 – often 3 – almost always	What can I do to move to the next level?
I recognize that continuing to learn at every opportunity enhances my ability to help others and cultivates my expertise and credibility.		
I realize the important value to being an understanding person who makes it a habit to listen to others empathically, therefore, deepening my ability to advise, motivate and guide.		
I acknowledge the value of physical fitness to be able to accomplish the work I need to do, and I will live a healthy lifestyle of exercise, rest, and nutrition.		
I understand I am nothing without the guidance of the Lord Jesus Christ. Daily meditation and scriptures make me aware of His presence and direction.		

EMPOWERING AND MOTIVATING OTHERS		
	At what level am I? 0 – not at all 1 – somewhat 2 – often 3 – almost always	What can I do to move to the next level?
I look for the unseen talents and abilities in those I mentor; I treat them with the respect these abilities deserve, and I give responsibilities that encourage growth.		
I am a life model for those around me by executing the habits of personal development in a manner that builds and exemplifies trust.		

SKILLSET	Examining Leadership		
TOOL	Keepers of the Light		
IMPACT	✓ Individual	✓ Team	✓ Group
PURPOSE	To assess personal leadership skills to be a "Keeper of the Light" (Lighthouse)		

DESCRIPTION

- Using a graphic of a lighthouse (provided), state the organization's mission and values.

- Ask individuals to identify their own personal qualities that align with and contribute to the organization's mission and values.

- Participants write each of their identified personal qualities on the lighthouse graphic in the spaces provided.

DEBRIEF

? What are the characteristics of individuals that contribute to the organization's mission and values?

? Why is alignment of individuals' qualities with organizational mission and values important?

MATERIALS

✓ Graphic of a lighthouse with the mission and values of the organization on it with spaces for adding individuals' personal qualities — one per participant

. . . .

If one advances confidently in the direction of their dreams, and endeavors to lead a life which they have imagined, they will meet with a success unexpected in common hours. ~

HENRY DAVID THOREAU, AMERICAN AUTHOR, POET, AND PHILOSOPHER

. . . .

Insert the Organization's Mission at the top of the lighthouse

Insert Organizational Values around the beams of light

Individuals write their personal qualities in the lighthouse structure

SKILLSET	Examining Leadership		
TOOL	Personal Action Plan Reflection Guide		
IMPACT	✓ Individual	Team	Group
PURPOSE	To identify goals and develop a plan of action to reach the goals		

DESCRIPTION

- Prepare a Personal Action Plan (PAP) by developing annual goals based on the four universal needs identified by Stephen Covey (2004). The plan should include measurable goals complete with a timeline for successfully achieving the goals.

  - ∾ Physical - To Live
  - ∾ Mental - To Learn
  - ∾ Emotional - To Love
  - ∾ Spiritual - To Leave a Legacy

- Develop a timeframe for reflecting upon progress made on the PAP. Consider incorporating monthly, quarterly, and annual reflection periods. More frequent reflection sessions are recommended early in the process.

- Allow a set time to reflect upon and internalize your experiences in a meaningful way and ultimately develop a lifetime habit of "disciplined reflection."

- Make and keep promises made to yourself in the PAP to increase your capacity to make and keep larger promises, thereby increasing the space between stimulus and response.

- The PAP Reflection Guide can be used to assist in directing the reflective process.

DEBRIEF

? Consider consulting with a trusted colleague as an accountability partner.

MATERIALS

✓ None

ADAPTED FROM
Covey, S. R. (2004) *The 8th habit: From effectiveness to greatness.* Houston: Free Press.

PAP REFLECTION GUIDE

PHYSICAL
- *Good Nutrition* - Do I have a balanced nutritious diet?

- *Consistent Balanced Exercise* - Do I have a consistent, balanced exercise routine?

- *Rest* - Am I getting sufficient rest?

- *Reflection* - Am I allowing time for silent reflection?

- *Relaxation* - Am I allowing time for relaxation?

- *Preventive Thinking* - Am I focusing on what I need to do when I do not feel well or focusing on what I need to do to remain well?

MENTAL
- *Continuous, Systematic, Disciplined Study and Education* - Do I systematically allow time for intellectual growth?

- *Cultivate Self-Awareness* - What explicit strategies do I use to increase the space between stimulus and response?

- *Teach Learning to Others* - How do I internalize my learning by teaching it to others?

EMOTIONAL
- *Self-Awareness*

> Habit One - Be Proactive: How well do I exercise my freedom to choose?

- *Personal Motivation*

>   Habit Two - Begin with the End in Mind: What are my highest priorities, goals and values?

- *Self-Regulation*

>   Habit Three - Put First Things First, and

>   Habit Seven - Sharpen the Saw: Do I live by my priorities? Do I constantly renew myself?

- *Empathy*

>   Habit Five - Seek First to Understand: How do I transcend my own story and get into the hearts and heads of others?

- *Social Skills*

>   Habit Four - Think Win-Win

>   Habit Five - Seek First to Understand, and

>   Habit Six - Synergize: Do I think in terms of mutual benefit, strive for mutual understanding and seek creative cooperation?

SPIRITUAL

- *Integrity* - How do I educate my conscience? Do I obey my conscious?

- *Meaning and Voice* - What does my life situation ask of me now? What should I do in my present responsibilities, duties, and stewardships? What would be the wise action to take?

. . . .

Reflection is an active process whereby the professional can gain an understanding of how historical, social, cultural and personal experiences have contributed to professional knowledge and practice. ~ R. G. WILKINSON, BRITISH AUTHOR

. . . .

SKILLSET	Examining Leadership		
TOOL	Achieve My Dream		
IMPACT	✓ Individual	✓ Team	✓ Group
PURPOSE	To engage in meaning writing as a way to evaluate what is desired in life		

DESCRIPTION

- Lead the participants to identify their personal goals in life.

- Ask:

  - If you had NO barriers, what would you do?
  - What is keeping you from pursuing your goals?
  - Using the following format, write a goal statement:

    Verb, Measure, From X to Y, by When.

    Example: Make (verb) a career change (measure) from teacher to administrator (X to Y) within the next year (by when).

DEBRIEF

? Dialogue with participant and have him/her write the steps for accomplishing the identified goal. Make sure he/she includes the people to be involved, learning needed, resources to be acquired, etc.

MATERIALS

✓ A notebook to record reflective ideas, identify goals, and steps to accomplishing them.

✓ With a symbol (star, smiley face, check mark), note when a goal has been reached.

SKILLSET	Examining Leadership		
TOOL	The Prism		
IMPACT	✓ Individual	✓ Team	✓ Group
PURPOSE	To empower individuals by identifying the alignment among their ideal job, their present job, and their personal skill set		

DESCRIPTION

- Explain the function of a prism. (Prisms refract or bend light rays so that one beam of light will separate into a spectrum of colors.)

- Give each person a sheet of 8 ½ x 11 paper (or card stock). Instruct each participant to fold the paper into three equal parts.

- Label the parts as follows: Ideal Job, Present Job, Personal Skills

Ideal Job	Present Job	Personal Skills

- In the first section, have each participant identify the skills, knowledge, and experiences needed for his/her ideal job.

- In the middle section, have each participant identify the skills, knowledge, and experiences needed for his/her present job.

- In the third section, have each participant identify his/her skills, abilities, education, talents, etc.

- The paper can be taped together to form a triangular prism.

- With a trusted friend or colleague, have teams of two process the information on the three sections. Encourage the pairs to look for alignment, areas of need, etc.

DEBRIEF

? What might be the personal feeling when there is an obvious lack of alignment?

? What might a person do if there is better alignment with his/her personal skill set and his/her ideal job than with the present job?

? What might a person do if there is a glaring need in his/her skill set?

? What other considerations should be examined?

MATERIALS

✓ 8½ × 11 sheets of paper or cardstock for each participant

✓ Scotch tape

. . . .

In the long run the most important results of leadership are not what we achieve but what we become in that achieving.

~ BRENT FILSON, LEADERSHIP CONSULTANT AND AUTHOR

. . . .

SKILLSET	Examining Leadership		
TOOL	Pros and Cons		
IMPACT	✓ Individual	Team	Group
PURPOSE	To assist leaders in decision-making or evaluating opportunities		

DESCRIPTION

- Have the participants identify an opportunity or decision under consideration. Form it into a question: (e.g., What are the pros and cons if I accept this offer of employment? What are the pros and cons of implementing a new policy related to employee attendance?)

- Using a legal pad, have the participants write the opportunity or decision under consideration at the top of the page. Just below, draw a vertical line through the center of the page from the top to the bottom.

- On the left, write "Pros" as a heading and on the right, use "Cons" as the heading.

- Brainstorm and list the likely positive and negative aspects related to the consideration. Consider interests, strengths, personal fulfillment, family obligations, time factors, values, etc.

- Assign a numerical weight to each pro and con using 1, 3, or 5 with 5 carrying the heaviest weight.

- Total the results for the Pros and for the Cons.

- When the brainstorming list is complete and the weights have been assigned and totaled, encourage the participants to use the results to make judgments.

DEBRIEF

? When the brainstorming list is complete and the weights have been assigned and totaled, use the results to inform decision-making.

? For every pro, was there also a con?

MATERIALS

✓ Chart – provided

Issue to be considered:	
PROs	**CONs**

. . . .

In each of us are places where we have never gone.
Only by pressing the limits do you ever find them.
~ DR. JOYCE BROTHERS, AMERICAN PSYCHOLOGIST AND TV PERSONALITY

. . . .

SKILLSET	Examining Leadership		
TOOL	Self-Assessment and Commitment		
IMPACT	✓ Individual	✓ Team	Group
PURPOSE	To find areas of need for discussion to improve the individual, team or organization		

DESCRIPTION

- Explain that this activity focuses on the individual and his/her part on the team.

- Have participants respond to questions on the Self-Assessment sheet (provided) which are about things individuals may need to increase, decrease, improve, or approach in a different manner.

- Assure the group that the self-assessment is for each individual's information only, to increase self-awareness about ways to help the team or organization.

- Have each person take the self-assessment and write the name of a colleague who demonstrates that question well.

- Have the group choose three areas they most want to improve and brainstorm how to do so.

DEBRIEF

? How are these expectations met both individually and as a group

? What trends and insights have been learned?

? Who were the individuals that were selected as a good example of each question? Recognize the individuals who were named as good examples.

MATERIALS

✓ Copy of Self-Assessment sheet for each participant.

Adapted from: leadership-tools.com http://www.leadership-tools.com/team-buildling-ideas.html

Self-Assessment		
	Self-rating Low – 1 High – 5	Who exemplifies this quality?
Do I fully participate in team meetings?		
Do I demonstrate a positive attitude?		
If I have an issue, do I deal with it directly with that person rather than complaining to a third party?		
Do I listen openly to new ideas?		
Do I sincerely celebrate others' success?		
Do I follow through on anything I agree to do?		
Do I represent my team positively to non-team members?		
Do I willfully share the load?		
If facts are not clear, do I check for clarity rather than make assumptions?		
Do I look for opportunities to make others stars?		
Do I meet deadlines?		
Do I take the initiative to do whatever needs to be done?		

. . . .

The future belongs to those who believe in the beauty of their dreams. ~ ELEANOR ROOSEVELT, LONGEST-SERVING FIRST LADY OF THE U.S.

. . . .

SKILLSET	Examining Leadership		
TOOL	Self-Evaluation		
IMPACT	✓ Individual	Team	Group
PURPOSE	To evaluate basic needs, assess ways to satisfy them, and to set and reach goals		

DESCRIPTION

- Using the chart provided, write in each space what you are currently doing to satisfy each of the needs.

- In areas that are lacking, identify specific action for improvement (Goal). For each goal, establish a reasonable action plan including completion date.

- Meet bi-weekly or weekly with an accountability partner to discuss progress being made in each of these areas and to evaluate the level of balance in life.

- As goals are met, new goals should be established making this an ongoing self-evaluation process.

DEBRIEF

? Embedded in activity

MATERIALS

✓ Chart – several for each participant to use and update as information changes

Mind – To Learn	Heart – To Love
What Currently Doing: Goal: Action Plan:	What Currently Doing: Goal: Action Plan:
Body – To Live	**Spirit – To Leave a Legacy**
What Currently Doing: Goal: Action Plan:	What Currently Doing: Goal: Action Plan:

....

The ultimate defense against growing old is your dream. Nothing is as real as a dream. Your dream is the path between the person you are and the person you hope to become. Success isn't money. Success isn't power. The criteria for your success are to be found in your dream, in yourself. Your dream is something to hold on to. It will always be your link with the person you are today, young and full of hope. If you hold on to it, you may grow old, but you will never be old, and that is the ultimate success.

~ TOM CLANCEY, AMERICAN AUTHOR OF ESPIONAGE STORIES

....

SKILLSET	Examining Leadership		
TOOL	Strengths & Passion		
IMPACT	✓ Individual	Team	Group
PURPOSE	To assess personal strengths with passion		

DESCRIPTION

Using the Strengths and Passions Worksheet (provided), have participants identify their personal passions and talents/gifts, and assess how the two align.

- Step One: Identify Your Passions

  - Populations
  - Sectors
  - Passion

- Step Two: Identify Your Talents/Gifts/Strengths

  - Assess your gifts, talents, and strengths and how they are aligned with your passions.

- Step Three: Analyze Your Job Description (or Desired Job)

  - Examine the relationship between your gifts, talents, and strengths and your job description or desired job.

DEBRIEF

? Do you have the skills required for the job? If not, is retraining feasible?

? Will your talents/gifts/strengths be useful to the job?

? Do you enjoy working with the people at the job? Do you enjoy working with a few or many?

? Are you comfortable in the environment?

? What satisfaction/fulfillment do you receive from your job?

? Which passions can you engage in the job?

? Do your talents/gifts/skills and passion align with the job?

MATERIALS

✓ Maintain a reflection journal as you participate in this activity.

✓ Worksheet – one per participant

....

Personal leadership is the process of keeping your vision and values before you and aligning your life to be congruent with them.

~ STEPHEN COVEY, LEADERSHIP CONSULTANT AND WRITER

....

STRENGTHS AND PASSIONS WORKSHEET

Step One: *Identify Your Passions*

- **Populations**—With what populations (infants, children, teens, veterans, homeless, aging, etc.) do you enjoy working?

  _____

  _____

- **Sectors**—In what type of environment or system (education, business, arts, etc.) do you feel most comfortable and vital?

  _____

  _____

- **Passion**—What issues (education, environment, hunger, peace, poverty, specific disease, a specific country, a specific talent or skill) call you to action?

  _____

  _____

Step Two: *Identify Your Talents/Gifts/Strengths*

- Make a list of your gifts, talents, and strengths:
- Identify how your gifts/talents/strengths align with the passions you identified above.

Step Three: *Analyze Your Job Description (or Desired Job)*

- What skills are required for the job?
- Who are the people you work with in the job?
- What is the environment in the job?
- Does the job provide satisfaction with fulfillment?
- Are there opportunities to engage your passions?

SKILLSET	Examining Leadership		
TOOL	Personal Alignment Tracking		
IMPACT	✓ Individual	Team	Group
PURPOSE	To assess the importance and time allotted to tasks		

DESCRIPTION

- In a small notebook, list all activities you engage in during the day as well as the length of time of engagement in the activity.

- After the first day, review the log and reflect on these questions:
    - ∞ What was the most important?
    - ∞ What took the most time?
    - ∞ What seemed to be most important at the time?
    - ∞ What was unimportant, the biggest waste of time?
    - ∞ How much time was spent on each activity?

- Compare how much time was spent on important, less important, and unimportant activities.

- Consider what makes a person productive in the organization.

- Set goals for the next day and repeat the exercise.

Note: After a period of daily review, this activity may become effective in a weekly review.

DEBRIEF

? Periodical debriefs between you and your mentor should be scheduled. (Although working with a mentor is desirable, this activity, even without a mentor, is worthwhile.)

MATERIALS

✓ Small notebook

....

In each of us are places where we have never gone. Only by pressing the limits do you ever find them. ~ DR. JOYCE BROTHERS

....

SKILLSET	Examining Leadership		
TOOL	Targeting Values		
IMPACT	✓ Individual	✓ Team	Group
PURPOSE	To identify what is most important to accomplish their jobs		

DESCRIPTION

- Distribute a template or hand-drawn dart board (target) to each participant (provided). The target should consist of at least five concentric circles large enough to write inside.

- Have participants identify an area of their career or work responsibilities to examine as they consider their values.

- Participants should identify five values that they consider as very important.

- Participants should review each value individually and assign one of the following ratings within the circle:

  - Outer circle - Not at all important (in my career, to this assignment, to my organization, to our stakeholders)
  - Next - Not very important (in my career, etc.)
  - Middle Circle - Moderately important (in my career, etc.)
  - First Circle from Center - Very important (in my career, etc.)
  - Bull's Eye - Essential (in my career, etc.)

- After review, individuals should assess whether or not their values are in alignment with their work. As appropriate, individuals may discuss their findings with a partner or in small groups.

DEBRIEF

? What does this tell me about my commitment to the organization?

? What can be done to align my goals better with those of the organization?

MATERIALS

✓ Dart board graphic (target) for each participant

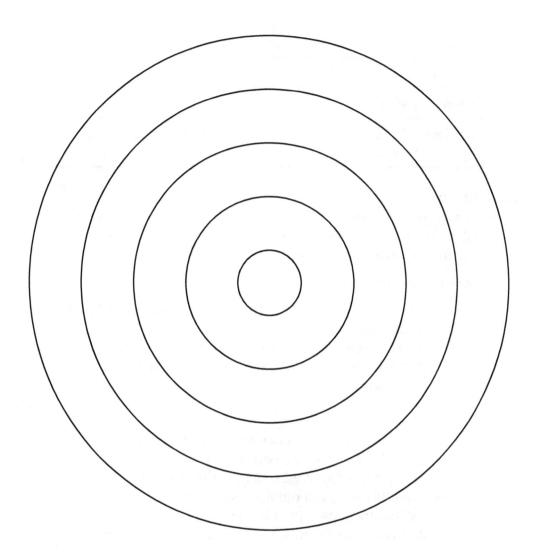

ADAPTED FROM
Career Development Center, Binghamton University, State University
of New York.

....

There are many things in life that will catch your eye, but
only a few will catch your heart...pursue those. ~ ANONYMOUS

....

SKILLSET	Examining Leadership		
TOOL	Vision Check		
IMPACT	✓ Individual	Team	Group
PURPOSE	To stay on track, stay motivated, keep perspective, and identify and respect the priorities in life		

DESCRIPTION

- Instruct the participant to consider priorities and tasks/projects that are his/her assignments and to conduct a weekly "vision check'" applying techniques from a medical vision check:

Check current prescription:

- ⤷ Identify the 4–5 "letters" (priorities/tasks/projects) that are most important this week.
- ⤷ Ask: How clearly can I see them? Has my E turned into a P? (Meaning: Have other circumstances changed what I am viewing?)

Check lens:

- ⤷ Just as when the eye doctor puts the lenses in front of you and asks "Can you see better with A or B?" and flips the lens, practice looking at each "letter" through a different lens.
- ⤷ Does this situation require a look through a political lens, a structural lens, a people lens, or a symbolic lens? (See Bolman & Deal's (2008) *Reframing Organizations*)

Check new prescription:

- ⤷ After the exam, the physician indicates if a new prescription is needed.
- ⤷ To parallel, prescribe specific actions to take related to each of the "letters" this week.
- ⤷ Remove any "letters" that are no longer priorities.
- ⤷ Maintain "letters" that are priorities for next week.

DEBRIEF
? Embedded in activity

MATERIALS
✓ Notebook

REFERENCE
Bolman, L., & Deal, T. (2008). *Reframing organizations: Artistry, choice, and leadership*. San Francisco: Jossey-Bass.

....

The very essence of leadership is that you have to have a vision. It's got to be a vision you articulate clearly and forcefully on every occasion. You can't blow an uncertain trumpet. ~ REVEREND THEODORE M. HESBURGH, PRIEST AND PRESIDENT EMERITUS OF NOTRE DAME

....

ANCHORS

....

Before becoming an effective organizational leader you must decide whether or not your life's purpose is to assume the mantle of leadership.

Effort and courage are not enough without purpose and direction.

~JOHN F. KENNEDY, 35TH U.S. PRESIDENT

Everyone has a unique purpose in life. Deciding whether or not your driving purpose is leadership requires defining your personal mission, assessing your beliefs and attitudes, developing your skills, and aligning your purpose with those of the organization. This is accomplished by embracing a mindset of continual reflection. The importance of purpose received similar affirmation fromDiscover Your Destiny by Peel and Peel (1996) in which they stated, "We believe our God-given destiny is also where our deepest joy lies" (p. 14).

Focusing on mission and purpose, Leider (1997) used the term "a calling." He stated:

> A calling is about working with meaning and joy and a sense of contributing to the greater community. A calling means bringing spirit and livelihood back together again. A calling calls forth the deeper questions of work such as how, why, and for whom we do our work...(p. 77).

He continued:

> Most of us want to feel that we are significant and that our work calls us to something enduring and worthwhile. More than anything else, good work enables us to spend our precious time in ways that are consistent with our calling in life. (p. 81)

Matusak (1997) suggested that the most important work of leadership is developing self. When discussing Perry Smith's writing, *Taking Charge,* Matusak stated, "The quest for leadership is primarily an inner journey to discover our true selves, which include our strengths, skills, prejudices, and talents, and a recognition of our unique gifts and some of our limitations" (p. 17). Similarly, Parrott (2006) explained that before individuals can lead others, they must be trustworthy enough to lead themselves, an inside-out approach, to hold themselves accountable to their "true and best." Covey (2004) spoke of the necessity of private victory preceding public victory and emphasized the importance of leading one's self before being able to lead others. He also discussed the importance of beginning with the end in mind, finding and pursuing your mission in life.

The beliefs you as a prospective leader hold are essential to effective leadership. As you consider leadership, assess your qualities in light of good reasons for choosing leadership. The *good reasons* suggested by Teatro (2013) include:

- desiring to change things for the better;

- having a genuine interest in other people and in working as a team;

- believing in the coaching, teaching process that communicates well and builds relationships; and

- understanding that people watch you, do what you do and say what you say, so modeling with integrity and being accountable are essential.

....

There are no short cuts to "being the best"; it always involves big dream and the unwavering commitment to pay the price through discipline and hard work. ~ANONYMOUS

....

Leadership is not so much about a position you hold but is about integrity and the desire to serve. In an article in *The Leader of the Future,* Kouzes and Posner (1997) named the following lessons as essentials for potential leaders:

1. Leaders don't wait. (Leaders must have a sense of urgency and be proactive.)

2. Character counts. (Leaders must be viewed as having integrity and credibility.)

3. Leaders have their heads in the clouds and their feet on the ground. (Leaders must be forward looking with a sense of direction and vision for the future and be aware of present realities.)

4. Shared values make a difference. (Leaders must be able to build a community of shared values.)

5. Leaders can't do it alone. (Leaders must enlist others to fulfill the mission.)

6. The legacy a leader leaves is the life s/he leads. (Leaders must show up, pay attention, participate directly in the business of getting things done, and show by example that they are committed to the aspirations they espouse. In other words, 'Do what you say you will do.')

7. Leadership is everyone's business. (Leaders must involve others in working toward organizational goals. When the leader in everyone is liberated, extraordinary things happen.)

When you choose to become a leader, you must consider when to assume a formal leadership role. The answer, put simply, is when your education, background, maturity, and skills give evidence of a foundational preparedness to assume greater responsibility. Only then should the challenge of assuming a formal leadership role begin.

Green (2002) contributed to an article in Forbes magazine entitled "Top 5 Leadership Skills for Sustained Innovation." He recommended developing the following skills:

1. Challenge assumptions: Shed old ideas and ways of thinking.

2. Change perspectives: Focus attention on what could be, not on what is or what was.

3. Ask the right question: Ask questions that project the future as if it were the present to shift people's attention from why something cannot be done to what can be done to achieve it.

4. Question the right answer: Forget about finding THE right answer; focus on identifying multiple solutions, then choose the best or combination thereof to support goals. "Good often gets in the way of great" (p. 2).

5. Stop jumping to solutions: Ask 'what if' questions to move beyond the obvious solution.

In his seminal work, *Good to Great*, Collins (2001) gave the image of getting the right people on the right bus and in the right seats. He explained the importance of aligning the skills and talents of people with the organization's purpose and placing them in the right job functions for optimal effectiveness. At times, this could even mean helping individuals to locate positions in other organizations for which they are better suited. An individual whose personal mission does not align with the mission of the organization in which they work remains unfulfilled. Jones (1996) insisted that the most important thing a person can do is to find one's mission and then accomplish it. Not only is this critical for the personal fulfillment of individuals but also for the success of organizations.

There is one art of which every [person] should be master: the art of reflection.

~ S. T. COLERIDGE, 18TH-19TH CENTURY ENGLISH POET

Those in leadership know that the habit of personal assessment is important. This is done through a process of reflection. Although not necessarily a formal written activity, time must be allotted for the process. To fulfill your mission, reflection is essential to your ongoing development as a leader.

Staropoli (2000) asserted that reflection is a leadership fundamental. He wrote:

> Reflection, broadly defined here, is stepping back from the window and observing: noting what is happening, looking for patterns, and looking for meaning. It's a thought process, an emotional process, an intuitive process all at once. Reflection, as I use it here, is more active than meditation or contemplation; and it is deeper and richer than thinking about something. It is a way to capture meaning, clarity, and direction in life. (p. 1)

Discussing the importance of reflection, Drucker (1974) recommended that leaders consider if they are spending their time and are asking others to engage in causes and commitments that are valuable, honest, and worthwhile to humanity.

Westpoint Colonel Eric Kail (2011) affirmed the important role of reflection when he said,

> The concept of reflection may sound self-involved but it is actually just the opposite. By not reflecting, we engage in a narcissistic rationalization that makes us feel better about the events in our lives yet keeps us from learning from them. There is a natural tendency to attribute all of our successes to ourselves and all our failures to forces beyond our control. (Para. 4)

Gaining wisdom from experience requires reflection. In thinking back on the significant events of my life, experiences good and bad, it was the act of assigning meaning that has made all the difference for me. Reflection requires a type of introspection that goes beyond merely thinking, talking or complaining about our experiences. It is an effort to understand how the events of our life shape the way in which we see the world, ourselves, and others. And it is essential for any leader. (Para. 2)

Cottrell (2010) suggested that reflection is helpful in the following ways:

- Making sense of experience: For learning to occur, reflecting on experience is required.

- Standing back: Stepping back makes possible a different view of experience.

- Repetition: Rerunning experience allows for more comprehensive insight.

- Deeper honesty: Making effort to get to the truth, even that which is difficult to admit.

- Weighing up: Using even handed judgment, weigh things in the balance.

- Clarity: Holding up a mirror to what has happened.

- Understanding: Learning at a deeper level.

- Making judgments: Draw conclusions based on reflective judgment.

She also explained that the purpose of reflection is to enable individuals to make connections, generate ideas, evaluate behaviors and make progress toward goals.

....

Leadership is practiced not so much in words as in attitude and in actions. ~ HAROLD S. GENEEN,
FORMER SENIOR VICE-PRESIDENT OF RAYTHEON

....

Socrates in Plato's *Apology* (1656) provided an appropriate capstone to the discussion of reflection. It is reported that when responding to charges before his execution for encouraging his students to challenge the thinking of the day, Socrates expressed, "The unexamined life is not worth living."

For people of faith especially, leadership will be viewed from a spiritual dimension. In recent years, in response to the frequency of leaders who have been charged with unethical practices in business, there has been an increase in leadership literature focusing on the spiritual aspects of authentic leadership. Hawkins and Parrott (2013) discussed the unique challenges that people of faith may have as leaders and warned that the pressures of leadership may challenge living authentically by spiritual principles. In addressing leadership as spiritual, they identified qualities of competent leaders and suggested an added dimension on each of eight qualities for competent leaders who are also authentically spiritual. The following chart summarizes these points.

Dimensions of Leaders Who are Competent	Added Dimensions of Competent Leaders Who are also Spiritual
Intentional in decisions and actions	Rely on faith to compel ethical decisions and act with integrity
Engage in self-reflection	Self-reflection leads to greater depth and insights
Self-assess	Are open to feedback and make corrections
Build healthy teams	Create faithful, trusting, respectful communities
Require intellectual integrity	Have courage to view/address the world as it is, not as they desire it to be
Require ethical integrity	Tell the truth, keep promises and raise the standard of ethical integrity
Serve their followers	Are servant leaders, treating workers with compassion, inspiring their best
Pursue personal/professional development	Know that leading depends on continuous learning, honing, and improving leadership

In summary, as an effective organizational leader, you need to be personally, professionally, and consistently reflective. Examining whether or not leadership is your calling is an inside-out process. IF you determine that leadership is your calling, certain things must occur:

- Define your personal mission.

- Ascertain if your mission aligns with that of the organization for which you work.

- Assure that your beliefs and attitudes support your mission and are exemplified through your daily walk and interactions.

- Develop continually knowledge and skills that will enable you to grow and to lead the growth of others.

- Embrace your spirituality and consistently live with integrity and in keeping with your ethical values and faith.

- Engaging in personal reflection fully encompasses this inside-out approach.

....

*Everyone has his own specific vocation or mission
in life...Therein he cannot be replaced, nor can his life
be repeated. Thus, everyone's task is as unique as
is his specific opportunity to implement it.*

~ VIKTOR FRANKL, AUSTRIAN PSYCHIATRIST AND HOLOCAUST SURVIVOR

....

Charting Direction

WHERE DO YOU WANT TO BE?

The navigational chart provides an environmental scan to assist the ship's captain in determining the best route to travel.

The job of a ship's captain, along with the navigational team, is to chart the course that will result in arrival to the designated place without danger to the ship, the crew, or the cargo. To navigate effectively, the ship's captain must find the answers to important considerations: What job is to be done to fulfill the purpose for which the ship has launched? (Purpose) What is the route to getting there? (Mission) How and where do we need to deliver the goods? (Vision/Destination) There are numerous navigational markers that the captain values to assist his efforts to avoid danger and fulfill the mission. The beacons from the lighthouse caution the captain to environmental conditions that may create crises or need for change in direction.

> *The two most important days in your life are the day you are born and the day you find out why.*
>
> ~MARK TWAIN

Similarly, in today's business world (corporate, education, religious organizations, non-profits, charity, etc.), although the purposes of organizations differ, each has to chart its unique course. Its mission is to deliver goods or services to the specific clientele, market, or audience in a way that values the employee, grows the company, and provides quality services or goods. Environmental and organizational scanning serve as lighthouse beacons to guide leaders in charting direction for the organization.

. . . .

Alice: Would you tell me, please, which way I ought to go from here?

The Cat: That depends a good deal on where you want to get to.

Alice: I don't much care where.

The Cat: Then it doesn't much matter which way you go.

> ~ LEWIS CARROLL, *ALICE IN WONDERLAND*

. . . .

TOOLS FOR CHARTING DIRECTION

SKILLSET	Charting Direction		
TOOL	Beginning the Dream		
IMPACT	Individual	✔ Team	Group
PURPOSE	To prioritize values		

DESCRIPTION

Note: Prior to the meeting, have a leadership team or an ad hoc team develop a list of 10 values that may represent the organization.

- Distribute the list of 10 preliminary values and have the whole team review the list, discuss any unspoken values, and add to or modify the list.

- Have the whole team prioritize each value and provide a brief rationale for the priority placed on each value.

- Have the whole team discuss the meaning and importance of each value, giving attention to the meaning of words.

- Instruct the whole team to consolidate the list and add any new words that represent a general consensus of the team. (This consolidation process may take more than one session to complete.)

- Assign an individual to collect the words, ideas, and rationale for choices into a document that represents the final draft.

- Instruct the core group to identify everyday situations that put the values to the test or require prioritizing one value against another.

- Lead the whole group in conducting a final discussion to get feedback and explore how these values apply in the everyday situations identified above.

- Have each team member write a 2-3 sentence paragraph describing the dream ending for the values: "I have a dream that one day...."

- Have volunteers from the team read their "I have a dream" paragraph to the entire group.

DEBRIEF

? How will these values be evident in the workplace?

? How do personal values impact organizational values?

? What are the ways that personal values can be different from organizational values?

? How will the public be able to see the values in action?

MATERIALS

✓ Prior to the full team meeting, the core group brainstorms and identifies a list of 10 (more or fewer as needed) preliminary values, starting with the organization's core values or beliefs.

✓ Prepare copies of list for the teams.

ADAPTED FROM:

Covey, S.R. (1989). *Principle-Centered Leadership*. Houston: Free Press.

· ·

Vision without action is but a dream. Action without vision passes but time. Vision with action can change the world.

~ JOEL BARKER, AMERICAN FUTURIST, AUTHOR AND FILM MAKER

· ·

SKILLSET	Charting Direction		
TOOL	Building Bridges		
IMPACT	Individual	✓ Team	Group
PURPOSE	To illustrate effective planning and teamwork		

DESCRIPTION

- Divide participants into teams of five.

- Give each team:

    - A stack of newspapers
    - Two rolls of masking tape
    - One large unopened can (e.g., juice, beef stew, approximately 12 oz.)

- Explain that the assignment is for each team to build a bridge that is *high enough* that the can will be able to pass under it in an upright position and be *strong enough* to hold the can on the bridge. Only the newspapers and masking tape may be used to build the bridge. The bridge cannot be supported by or leaned against or attached to anything else.

- Give 20 minutes for the bridge to be constructed. (Timing can be flexible according to the needs of the group.)

- When the time for building is over, have each group in turn test its bridge to see if it meets specifications. This is NOT a contest. Each group has the opportunity to be successful.

DEBRIEF

? What planning did your group do before you started building?

? Did the plan work as originated or were adjustments necessary?

? What roles did members of the group take?

? Did someone emerge as a leader recognized by the group?

? What type of leadership did the group have?

? How were decision made?

? What contributed to the success of the work?

MATERIALS

✓ Newspapers

✓ Masking tape

✓ 12 oz. (+/-) cans of stew, juice, etc.

SKILLSET	Charting Direction		
TOOL	Cup Stack		
IMPACT	Individual	✔ Team	✔ Group
PURPOSE	To work together to accomplish a difficult task without quitting or giving up when some get frustrated		

DESCRIPTION

- Divide participants into teams of 5–6 and distribute materials to each team.

- Challenge the teams to build a pyramid out of the paper cups (four on the bottom, three on the next row, then two, and finally one on the top).

- Explain that each team member should hold on to one of the strings that are attached to a rubber band. The team uses this device to pick up the cups and place them on top of each other (by pulling the rubber band apart and then bringing it back together over the cups.) If there are less than 6 people on a team, some team members may have to hold more than one string.

- Caution team members that they may not touch the cups with their hands or any other part of their bodies. Even if a cup falls to the floor, only the rubber band with strings may be used.

- If some teams finish before others, encourage them to become cheerleaders for teams still working.

DEBRIEF

? Was anyone frustrated during this activity? If so, how was it handled?

? Why was teamwork so important for this activity?

? Are you ever in a situation where you must use teamwork? Is this always easy for you? Why or why not?

? What skills are needed to be good at teamwork?

? Why is teamwork hard?

? What did you do today to contribute to your team?

MATERIALS

✓ Cut 6 pieces of string into 2–3 foot long pieces for each team of 6. Tie each piece of string to a rubber band as evenly spaced as possible so when finished it will be a rubber band with six pieces of string attached to it. (It should look like sunshine with six sun rays going out in all directions.)

✓ 10 paper cups of equal size placed upside down on the table, for each team

✓ 1 rubber band with 6 pieces of string attached, for each team

··

The greatest pleasure in life is doing what people say can't be done. ~ NORTHERN TRUST BUSINESS BANKING AD

··

SKILLSET	Charting Direction		
TOOL	From Values to Beliefs		
IMPACT	Individual	Team	✓ Group
PURPOSE	To have participants clarify values		

DESCRIPTION

- Ask participants to stand in the middle of the room to listen to value statements.

- Explain:
  - When a value statement is stated (see examples below) and the participant agrees, he/she is to move to the left of the leader.
  - When a statement is spoken to which individuals disagree, they are to move to the right of the leader.
  - A choice must be made for each statement. No one may remain uncommitted in the middle of the room.

- Conduct this activity for approximately 7 minutes.

DEBRIEF

? What did you learn about yourself during this activity?

? What did you learn about others?

? Was it difficult to demonstrate a difference of opinion with people you associate with most closely? Why or why not?

? Were there times when you felt it was unsafe to express your values?

? How can defining your values help to clarify your direction?

? How can defining values help clarify the organization's direction?

MATERIALS

✓ Create a list of statements that are customized to represent the values/beliefs of the organization.

Example Values Statements:

1. Everyone deserves medical care.

2. People are intrinsically good.

3. Insider trading is okay if no one finds out.

4. What the police don't know won't hurt them.

5. Taking a sick day when you are not sick is okay.

6. It is the teacher's responsibility to ensure that students are successful in school.

SKILLSET	Charting Direction		
TOOL	Get on Board		
IMPACT	Individual	✓ Team	Group
PURPOSE	To emphasize the importance of all team members supporting one another and working together		

DESCRIPTION:

- Randomly place 5 to 10 brightly colored 8 x 5 pieces of paper on the floor to represent logs on the river between the banks (marked off with string, tape, etc.).

- Explain to the group that:

  - They must cross the turbulent river using the logs as stepping stones.
  - Everyone must contribute to crossing the river.
  - When the first member leaves the bank to cross the river, every member must have physical contact with another member so that the entire team is connected with the first member leaving the river bank.
  - If someone falls in the river, the entire group must return to the bank.
  - The leader may remove or replace logs while the team is crossing the river.

- Also, explain that:

  - Before anyone begins to cross the river, the group must problem solve, develop strategies and goals.
  - The group has a time limit for strategizing and crossing the river. (Suggested time is 10 minutes.)
  - The goal is to have everyone safely on the other side of the river.

DEBRIEF

? What difficulties did you experience crossing the river?

? What complications arose from having to support each team member throughout the process of crossing the river?

? What implications does this activity have for people working together in organizations?

MATERIALS

✓ Prepare 'logs' from colored paper. (8 x 5 pieces of paper)

✓ Using available space, create an imaginary river on the floor between two physical objects representing the river banks. (Suggested distance is 10-20 feet.)

✓ Stopwatch

SKILLSET	Charting Direction		
TOOL	How Would Ghandi Do It?		
IMPACT	Individual	✓ Team	Group
PURPOSE	To consider different points of view when deciding how to address a goal or problem		

DESCRIPTION

- Divide a large group into teams of 6-8 participants and ask each team to select a facilitator and reporter.

- Place a copy of the goal or problem under consideration in front of each team.

- Post a list of famous people to serve as "consultants" for a brainstorming session. Make sure the consultants represent widely different points of view. If Patton is used, balance with someone such as Mother Teresa to get a wide range of ideas.

Possible Consultants:

- Mahatma Ghandi, Hindu Leader
- Ray Charles, Singer
- Pablo Picasso, artist/painter
- Madonna, Singer
- Albert Einstein, German Physicist
- Billy Graham, Minister
- Margaret Thatcher, British Prime Minister
- Fred Astair, Dancer
- Margaret Mead, Cultural Anthropologist
- Arnold Palmer, Pro Golfer
- Tim Tebow, Football Player
- Rick Pitino, Basketball Coach
- Mother Teresa, Catholic Nun in India
- Teddy Roosevelt, U.S. President
- General George Patton, U.S. Army
- Victor Frankl, Holocaust Survivor

- Let participants choose the name tent of the "consultant" they will represent and give them a few moments to identify major characteristics (philosophy, work, style, etc.) of the chosen consultant.

- After identifying the problem under consideration, ask each participant: "What would (consultant's name) recommend to address this problem?"

- Let participants give input from the "consultant's" point of view.

- After receiving input from "consultants," have the group synthesize ideas and identify specific ones to be used to address the problem.

DEBRIEF

? What was the value of looking at a problem from different perspectives?

? How can stepping into someone else's shoes improve problem solving?

MATERIALS

✓ Prepare copies of goals/problems for distribution to participants.

✓ Prepare a name tent for each "consultant."

ADAPTED FROM:

Kearny, L. (1994). *The facilitator's toolkit.* Amherst, MA: HRD Press.

. . . .

The people who get on in this world are the people who get up and look for the circumstances they want and if they can't find them, make them. ~ GEORGE BERNARD SHAW, IRISH PLAYWRIGHT AND CO-FOUNDER OF LONDON SCHOOL OF ECONOMICS

. . . .

SKILLSET	Charting Direction		
TOOL	Look in the Mirror		
IMPACT	Individual	✓ Team	✓ Group
PURPOSE	To help team members find their team's path, identify focus, and create a slogan		

DESCRIPTION

- Distribute 11 × 17 sheets of paper, one to each team.

- Ask participants to turn the paper to portrait position and write the name of the team vertically along the left side of the paper, one letter per line (e.g., Communication, Data Management, Financial, etc.) Example:

  - F
  - I
  - N
  - A
  - N
  - C
  - I
  - A
  - L

- Have the team identify a word that begins with each letter, one that accurately represents a quality for which the team wants to be known.

- When completed, have the team review the list of words and assess if the words accurately describe how participants would like for the team to be viewed.

- When the team is satisfied with the selection of words, have participants discuss possible brief slogans (or brands) that could be used to represent the team. By consensus, have each team make a choice.

- Encourage the team to discuss tasks/responsibilities that need to be implemented to engender the qualities described and set timelines for addressing each one.

- Have the team prepare a visual with the slogan in the center surrounded by the descriptors by which the team wants to be viewed.

- Each team posts the visual, and the entire group takes a museum walk (moving from chart to chart) until all participants have reviewed all charts.

DEBRIEF

? How does this activity inform the day-to-day operations of the team?

? Are there other words that would also enhance the ones already identified?

? Would other teams be able to identify the same descriptors?

MATERIALS

✓ 11 × 17 sheets of paper, one for each small group

✓ Markers

. . . .

Transmit your vision emotionally by gaining credibility, demonstrating passion, establishing relationships and communicating a felt need. Transmit it logically by confronting reality, formulating strategy, accepting responsibility, celebrating victory and learning from defeat.

~ JOHN MAXWELL, EVANGELICAL PASTOR, AUTHOR AND SPEAKER

. . . .

SKILLSET	Charting Direction		
TOOL	Creating a Mission Statement		
IMPACT	✓ Individual	✓ Team	Group
PURPOSE	To create a rough draft of a personal mission statement		

DESCRIPTION

- Explain that a good mission statement will:

  - Be inspiring, engaging, meaningful
  - Be specific, clear, succinct
  - Include your work and personal life
  - Focus on your talents and gifts
  - Encompass a lifetime of activities, be ongoing

- Share examples of mission statements:

  - Jesus said that his mission was *"that they may have life and that they may have it more abundantly."* (John 10:10 KJV) All of His activities flowed from that mission: turning water into wine, healing the sick, raising the dead, teaching, etc.
  - A personal mission statement of one of the authors: *"It is the mission of Ruth Y. Cox to seize every opportunity to teach by example with excellence and creativity."*

- Ask each participant to prepare a rough draft of a personal mission statement.

- Suggest the following outline (but it can take many forms):

  It is my mission to _____
  (verbs and/or verb phrases)

  (how) _____

  (to, for, or with) _____

DEBRIEF

Ask participants to reflect on their mission statements by considering the following questions:

? Is your statement definitive?

? Does it set you apart from other people?

? Is it concise?

? Is it actionable?

? Is it memorable?

MATERIALS
✓ None

....

I am not afraid of storms, for I am learning how to sail my ship. ~ LOUISA MAY ALCOTT

....

SKILLSET	Charting Direction		
TOOL	Readiness for Strategic Planning		
IMPACT	Individual	✓ Team	✓ Group
PURPOSE	To determine an organization's need and/or readiness to begin a visioning or strategic planning process		

DESCRIPTION

Note: The questionnaire can be administered to all or selected employees. Information obtained is best when participants' results are anonymous. Based on the scored results, the leadership team can determine the appropriate course of action for the visioning or strategic planning process. The best order for strategic planning is:

1. Defining Values

2. Developing Beliefs

3. Setting Vision

4. Determining Mission

5. Identifying Goals

6. Creating Action Plan

Directions for completing the questionnaire:

- If a statement has two parts and you would answer **Definitely** to one part but not the other, then choose the weaker response for that statement. (For example, in the first statement, you may be able to answer **Definitely** that your organization has a clear vision, but not that there is consensus about the vision. Your response then should be **Maybe/Not Sure** rather than **Definitely**.)

- Score your project or organization on each statement using

    - 1 = Definitely
    - 2 = Maybe/Not sure
    - 3 = Definitely Not

- Write the number for each response in the SCORE column. Add the scores in the SCORE column to obtain the Total Score.

- 20+: If your total is 20 or more, then your organization is ready for a visioning strategic planning process.

- 19–15: If your total is between 15 and 19, then your organization probably would benefit from a strategic planning process.

- 14–0: If your total is under 15, then your organization has a well-established and understood vision. There is no urgency in beginning a new visioning or strategic planning process.

MATERIALS
✓ Chart for each participant

ADAPTED FROM

CIVICUS Strategic Planning Toolkit. Retrieved from: http://www.civicus.org/new/media/Strategic%20Planning.pdf

Readiness for Strategic Planning Questionnaire			
Statement	Definitely (1)	Maybe or Not Sure (2)	Definitely Not (3)
Our organization has a clear vision of what it wants to achieve, and there is consensus around this vision.			
Value issues are often discussed in our organization, and there is agreement on these values.			
The current mission statement of our organization reflects clearly what the organization does, for whom, and why it is important.			
Our organization regularly reflects on its strengths and weaknesses and on the opportunities and threats in the environment.			
Our organization has clear goals and objectives for what it wants to achieve.			
Our organization finds it easy to prioritize, making a distinction between what it must do, what it should do, and what it would like to do.			
Our organization has clear indicators by which it measures the impact of its work.			
The way in which our organization is structured internally makes sense in terms of efficiency and effectiveness.			
The work done by our organization fits together coherently. The different areas of work fit well with one another.			
The external and internal contexts in which our organization operates are relatively stable, and there have been no major changes in the past year.			
TOTAL SCORE PER COLUMN			
GRAND TOTAL			

SKILLSET	Charting Direction		
TOOL	Sift, Sort, and Compose Vision		
IMPACT	Individual	✓ Team	Group
PURPOSE	To condense the ideas given by the total group into a succinct statement that is representative and can be supported by all		

DESCRIPTION

- Ask each team to select a team facilitator, scribe, and reporter.

- Have the participants read over the statements given, identify major themes, and write themes on a chart.

- Develop themes into 2–4 sentences that are comprehensive in nature and address:

  - Service to be provided
  - Interaction of people
  - Climate of the organizational

- Have the scribe write the draft on chart paper.

- Have the teams prepare and report the draft to the total group for consensus. (Consensus is not a vote. It is the agreement that this is something we can all live with and is in alignment with the direction of the organization.)

DEBRIEF

? Are there components of the drafts that are consistent in all drafts?

? What are the unique parts?

Note: Appoint an ad hoc team to work through the draft vision statements to formulate a potential statement to be brought to the whole group.

MATERIALS

✓ Chart Paper

✓ Markers

SKILLSET	Charting Direction		
TOOL	Strength Sort		
IMPACT	Individual	✓ Team	✓ Group
PURPOSE	To work together to identify strengths of team members and the overall organization and how the strengths contribute to immediate focus areas		

DESCRIPTION

- Divide the group into small teams. Have participants identify and discuss the five top strengths they believe the team or organization possesses. (Examples of strengths: productive/knowledgeable staff, marketing expertise, articulate presenters, strong teams, competent support staff, creative ideas, commitment of time/energy, expertise of specific individuals, etc.)

- Have participants identify and discuss three main areas of focus that have been decided for emphasis during the next identified time period (quarter, semester, year).

- List each focus area on a piece of chart paper and post on the wall.

- Have the entire group discuss the meaning of each word to assure that all participants have a clear understanding. (Examples of focus areas: improved communication, use of data, increased stakeholder participation/input, increased recruitment, program development, building relationships, relevance of product, improved advertisement, etc.)

- After consensus, encourage individual teams to select one strength and record it on a single sheet of paper written large enough for the entire group to see; then the team turns attention to the leader.

- Each team shows the strength written on their individual sheets, and the large group decides under which area of focus each strength should be posted.

DEBRIEF

? What patterns exist that can inform day-to-day operations?

? What recommendations for future direction should be made?

MATERIALS
- ✓ Chart paper
- ✓ Markers

....

Setting a goal is not the main thing. It is deciding how you
will go about achieving it. And staying with that plan.

~ TOM LANDRY, FORMER COACH OF DALLAS COWBOYS

....

SKILLSET	Charting Direction		
TOOL	Visioning		
IMPACT	Individual	✓ Team	✓ Group
PURPOSE	To create a plan to problem solve		

DESCRIPTION

- Divide a large group into smaller groups of 5–7.

- Distribute the scenario provided to each member of each group with written instructions and worksheet.

- Allot approximately 60 minutes for the work to be done. Explain that each group will:

  - Read and discuss the scenario.
  - Create a vision statement to address the problem.
  - Establish goals and define objectives.
  - Identify specific tasks and prioritize.
  - Indicate follow-up, measuring, and checking if what is required has been accomplished.

Scenario: You were recently hired as the distribution supervisor in a medium mail order company that is known for making excellent gift items. You oversee 20 employees who pick, pack, and ship about 3,000 orders per day. Each order is worth $65.00 on average and usually contains three items. An auditing program was started by your predecessor. You have studied the results and determined that the accuracy rate of all orders shipped is running at about 94%. About 4% of the orders shipped have the wrong quantity of items, while about 2% of the orders have the wrong product.

From past experiences and from what you have gleaned from publications, you believe that the accuracy rate should be at least 98%. Also, the president of your division recently stated that one of the top priorities is to reduce adjustments on orders by half this year. You know that many of the adjustments made at the warehouses are because the wrong item or quantity of items was shipped. Reflect on what you want the department to look like. Gather your team to discuss the following topics and create a chart that includes the decisions made for each:

  - VISION STATEMENT
  - GOALS (No more than 3)
  - OBJECTIVES

       ❧ SPECIFIC TASKS & INDIVIDUALS/GROUPS RESPONSIBLE

       ❧ TIMELINES

       ❧ MEASUREMENTS

       ❧ FOLLOW-UP REQUIRED

DEBRIEF

? Are the items developed representative of the organization?

? What are the priorities needed in order to accomplish what has been identified?

? What will the organization have to do – or stop doing – in order to complete the goals identified?

? How does this relate to our organization?

? What can be learned from this activity?

MATERIALS

✓ Chart paper

✓ Markers

✓ Copies of scenario for each team

SKILLSET	Charting Direction		
TOOL	It's Your Bid		
IMPACT	Individual	✓ Team	✓ Group
PURPOSE	To collaborate to identify values of the organization		

DESCRIPTION

- Assign participants to teams as appropriate. Give each team a packet of play money.

- Have each team identify a spokesperson and 3–5 values for the organization or project, write them on large tablet paper, and post them on the wall for all to see.

- Have teams walk around the room viewing the charts and deciding how much of the team's money they are willing to bid in order to see specific values as a priority.

- Begin the bidding process by going through the list of values and having each team's spokesperson submit the team's bid.

- After all values have been considered for bids, rank the list to identify the values prioritized by the group.

DEBRIEF

? What was the process your team used in prioritizing the values?

? Did the team place money on values other than those submitted by their team?

? How did this activity help your team prioritize values?

FOLLOW-UP AT A LATER MEETING

? What were the top priorities as identified in the activity?

? Do the values accurately reflect how the organization is currently functioning?

? What needs to be changed in the organization to reflect these values?

MATERIALS

✓ Large chart paper

✓ Markers

✓ Play money (8 - $500; 10 - $100; 10 - $50) per team (can be adjusted as desired)

SOURCES FOR LISTS OF VALUES

www.stevepavline.com/articles/list-of-values.htm

www.mindtools.com.Decision Making

SKILLSET	Charting Direction		
TOOL	Show Me		
IMPACT	Individual	✓ Team	✓ Group
PURPOSE	To embrace past accomplishments based on the organization's mission and explore future activities		

(Note: Most often, leaders are assigned to organizations that have already established written mission statements. It is important to honor the past and yet move the organization into the future.)

DESCRIPTION

- Group participants into teams equal to the number of phrases in the mission statement.

- Have each team validate the assigned phrase to "Show Me" how that phrase was implemented in the organization last year. Challenge the team to find five to eight illustrations of actual events.

- Next, have each team, using the same phrase, "Show Me" how that part of the mission could be improved, expanded, deepened, etc. in the next year. Encourage teams to identify four to six possibilities.

- Have each team report to the whole group. Keep the reporting in the order of the actual mission statement.

DEBRIEF

? What are the highlights from the past year?

? Was the mission overt in the workplace? If not, how could that be improved?

? What might be the top possibility for the next year, if done well, that would make the biggest difference in the organization?

? If appropriate, how many participants can recite or paraphrase the organization's mission?

MATERIALS

✓ Mission statement (See samples provided).

✓ Chart paper

✓ Markers

✓ Prior to the meeting, divide the established mission statement into phrases. See example. Write each phrase on a separate piece of chart paper.

AmerisourceBergen

Corporate Headquarters, 1300 Morris Drive, Suite 100, Chesterbrook, PA 19087

Mission Statement:

To build shareholder value by delivering pharmaceutical and healthcare products, services and solutions in innovative and cost effective ways. We will realize this mission by setting the highest standards in service, reliability, safety and cost containment in our industry. (http://www.missionstatements.com/fortune_500_mission_statements.html)

Mission separated into phrases:

To build shareholder value by delivering
pharmaceutical and healthcare products,
(in innovative and cost effective ways)
services (in innovative and cost effective ways)
solutions (in innovative and cost effective ways)

We will realize this mission by setting the
highest standards in service,
(highest standards in) reliability,
(highest standards in) safety and
(highest standards in) cost containment in our industry.

CSX Corporation

500 Water St., 15th Floor, Jacksonville, FL 32202

Mission Statement:

To be the safest, most progressive North American railroad, relentless in the pursuit of customer and employee excellence. (http://www.missionstatements.com/fortune_500_mission_statements.html)

Mission separated into phrases:

To be the safest (railroad),
most progressive North American railroad,
relentless in the pursuit of customer (excellence)
and employee excellence.

Trevecca Nazarene University

333 Murfreesboro Pike, Nashville, TN 37210

Mission Statement:

Trevecca Nazarene University is a Christian community providing education for leadership and service. (http://www.trevecca.edu/about/mission-and-goals)

Mission separated into phrases:

Trevecca Nazarene University is
> a Christian community
> providing education for leadership
> and (providing education for) service.

Sample chart:

Trevecca Nazarene University is a Christian community...

"Show me" how this was exemplified last year:

1

2

3

4

5

Show me how this could be expanded, improved, etc. next year:

1

2

3

4

5

6

ANCHORS

....

As an effective organization leader, you must begin your work by charting direction. This requires you to have a clear vision and effectively communicate with coworkers the importance of mission, purpose, goals, and objectives.

A variety of terms have been used when writing or speaking about charting direction. In his work *The Four Roles*, Stephen Covey (2002) identified the term as "Pathfinding." George Barna (1992) and Joel Barker (1990) each entitled a related work *The Power of Vision*. In his famous speech, Martin Luther King, Jr. (1963) stated "I have a dream." As leader of the civil rights movement, his actions lived out this vision. Lee Bolman and Terrance Deal (2008) suggested in *Reframing Organizations* that leaders should view organizational decisions through four frames: structural, human resource, political, and symbolic. Management Consultant Karl Albrecht (1994) wrote that leaders must have "bifocal vision," meaning they must be able to see the future ("far-sighted") and yet see the next step ("near-sighted").

To accomplish great things, we must not only act but also dream, not only plan but also believe.

~ ANATOLE FRANCE, FRENCH POET, JOURNALIST, AND NOVELIST

When charting direction, mission, vision, and action must be central to decision-making. There is nothing more powerful than the combination of mission and vision when it informs action. A noted futurist, Barker (1990) in the film *The Power of Vision* explained that "Vision without action is but a dream. Action without vision passes but time. Vision with action can change the world."

Heifezt (1994) developed the analogy of the balcony and the dance floor to discuss the importance of vision and action combined. Parrott (2007) discussed the dance floor metaphor when he said: "On the dance floor, you are expected to make wise decisions and implement the decisions effectively" (p. 15). In the balcony, you are expected to scan the total environment to "figure out what to do next in order to build the organization you envision" (p. 15). Parrott expanded the metaphor by referring to pausing on the stairs, a place and time to reflect on one's purpose and balance in life: "Beyond the dance floor and the balcony, you need to pause on the stairs. You need to remember and hold tightly to the life you want to create. At the core, good leadership is grounded in authenticity, leading true to your best" (p. 16).

Elected in 1960, President John F. Kennedy believed that America's confidence needed a boost because of the Soviets' accomplishments in space. On May 25, 1961, he delivered a message to Congress about "urgent national needs." He requested an appropriation of $7 to $9 billion over the coming five years for the U.S. space program, saying that "this nation should commit itself to achieving the goal, before the decade is out, of landing a man on the moon and returning him safely to the earth" (Para. 4) President Kennedy expressed this dramatic goal to focus attention on the nation's lagging space program. Although skeptics questioned if the National Aeronautics and Space Administration (NASA) could meet the challenge, within a year, two Americans, Alan Shepard and Gus Grissom, were the first to travel into space. This accomplishment is a strong example of a leader who charted a direction, provided resources, and presented a challenge that gave the impetus to competent subordinates to achieve the clearly stated goal.

To be effective when charting direction, you as a leader must consider the following: Why are we doing what we are doing? (Purpose)

- Where is our final destination? (Vision)

- What will guide us? (Values/Beliefs)

- How will we reach the destination? (Mission)

- Who is part of planning? (Leadership)

- When will each occur? (Action)

Creating Authenticity

WHAT CAN YOU DO TO DEVELOP A TRUSTING ENVIRONMENT?

The captain's hat signifies that the captain possesses the characteristics to fulfill the responsibilities of the job, to model leadership, and to inspire mutual trust.

A priority of the ship's captain is to build a community of trust and authenticity. The captain must embrace the leadership role and demonstrate the qualities expected of a leader. This is accomplished by modeling *competence, character, compassion,* and *courage.*

The two most important days in your life are the day you are born and the day you find out why.

~MARK TWAIN

The captain must possess a knowledge base of seamanship, navigation, and operations of the total ship to demonstrate *competence* to lead. *Character* is shown when leaders know who they are and act with integrity. As the crew sees the captain's work and life consistently reflecting values and beliefs, they will view their leader as a person of principle who is transparent and trustworthy. *Compassion* is reflected in the value the captain places on the crew, their personal circumstances, their abilities, and need for growth. All three of these — *Competence, Character* and *Compassion* — are demonstrated through *Courage* — the moral strength to hold self and others accountable and to make the tough decisions for the right reasons at the right time.

Most organizational leaders are appointed or "bubble up" from the ranks. They gain positions because they have demonstrated a knowledge base of the company's needs, operations, and direction (Competence). To be effective in the long-run, leaders must be respected by employees in the organization. This respect comes as a result of living consistently true to one's values, beliefs and principles — in other words, "walking your talk" (Character). Another essential quality is for the leader to show genuine concern for those who work in the organization (Compassion). And, the leader must have the moral strength to be self-disciplined, to make difficult decisions, and to hold co-workers accountable for their own abilities, attitudes, and production (Courage). As the light from the lighthouse provides guidance to the captain and the crew, these four qualities (Competence, Character, Compassion, Courage) serve as directional beacons for organizational leaders.

TOOLS FOR CREATING AUTHENTICITY

SKILLSET	Creating Authenticity		
TOOL	Banana Split		
IMPACT	Individual	✔ Team	✔ Group
PURPOSE	To illustrate the need to trust leaders		

DESCRIPTION

- Inform the participants that the objective of the activity is to create a banana split with various toppings.

- Prepare the ingredients for the standard banana split (banana, ice cream, syrup, toppings, whipped cream, etc.) AND ingredients that DO NOT belong, (catsup, gravy, mashed potatoes, etc.). Demonstrate how the leader will give the directions to make the banana split using only the traditional ingredients. (The "employees" are not in the room and are blindfolded.)

- The "employees" are brought in and seated at the table at which all ingredients are placed - both the standard ingredients and the additional ingredients. The leader begins systematically to give the directions as previously demonstrated giving care to replicate the instructions as in the demonstration. After the banana split has been constructed, the blindfold is removed.

DEBRIEF

? What was the degree to which the employees had to "trust" the leader?

? How specific and logical were the instructions needed to complete the task?

? What was the need to have the right materials available?

? How important is it to separate the appropriate ingredients from the "extra"?

? What were the motives of the leader in regard to the success or failure of the employees?

POSSIBLE EXTENSION:

Provide a banana split bar for the group to enjoy after the activity.

Note: This can be done with any basic food dish. If food cannot be used, Legos or building blocks can be used to create a structure as instructed by the leader.

MATERIALS
- ✓ Various ingredients for a banana split
- ✓ Additional food items (catsup, gravy, mashed potatoes, etc.)
- ✓ Bowls
- ✓ Spoons for each ingredient
- ✓ Aprons for each employee
- ✓ Clean up supplies (paper towels, etc.)

SKILLSET	Creating Authenticity		
TOOL	Follow the Leader		
IMPACT	Individual	✓ Team	✓ Group
PURPOSE	To illustrate how leaders and followers collaborate		

DESCRIPTION

- Have the team or group gather in a circle standing. Ideal size is 8–16 people. Tell everyone to face toward the middle of the circle.

- Choose one member as the "guesser" and have him/her briefly leave the room. While gone, choose a leader and tell the others they are to follow whatever movements the leader starts. Instruct them to all begin by swinging their arms in a circular motion when the guesser returns. At some point the leader will begin a new movement which the others are to follow. (The leader can do almost any gesture or movement that is appropriate.) The participants are to be careful not to reveal who the leader is. The objective is for the participants to prevent the "guesser" from identifying the leader.

- The guesser is allowed three (3) guesses as to who the leader is. If he/she is correct, the leader becomes the guesser. If he/she is incorrect, the leader is identified and another guesser is chosen and sent out of the room at which time a new leader is selected.

- Continue for a few rounds. Do not elongate the activity.

DEBRIEF

? How can different people lead without official titles?

? What is the importance of understanding the timing of activities?

? What was the importance of each person watching for subtle changes?

? What is the importance of employees seeing behaviors before they can model them?

? What impact does it have on an organization when an outsider cannot identify the leader?

? What is the moral of this activity? (The leader must show the way but the team members must pay attention.)

MATERIALS
✓   None

ADAPTED FROM:
http://www.group-games.com/action-games/follow-the-leader.htm

SKILLSET	Creating Authenticity		
TOOL	Mine Field		
IMPACT	Individual	✓ Team	✓ Group
PURPOSE	To illustrate the need to trust leaders		

DESCRIPTION

- Use a large empty indoor or outdoor space — approximately 20' × 20'. Mark the parameters of the "minefield" using tape, rope, etc. Scatter various objects in the space to create an obstacle course (mine field).

- In pairs, one person (leader) verbally guides his/her partner (employee) through the mine field. The employee is blindfolded without seeing the arrangement of objects in the minefield. This can be done with one person demonstrating, or as several teams working concurrently.

- Allow approximately 8–10 minutes for the team/s to move through the minefield. Rearrange objects if the activity is repeated the second time.

DEBRIEF

? How did trust between partners impact the success of the team?

? What are the consequences when minefields are encountered, personally and organizationally?

? What are minefields in the organizations?

? How can organizations work to remove mine fields?

MATERIALS

✓ Blindfolds

✓ Objects to create the minefield (Frisbees, plastic garbage can, plastic laundry baskets, etc. Make sure obstacles will not cause an injury when employee bumps into them.)

✓ Tape, rope, etc. to mark off mine field

....

The truth is that trust rules. Trust rules; your personal credibility, your ability to get things done, your team's cohesiveness, and your organization's innovativeness and performance. ~ JAMES KOUZES AND BARRY POSNER, *AUTHORS OF THE LEADERSHIP CHALLENGE*

....

SKILLSET	Creating Authenticity		
TOOL	Mirror, Mirror		
IMPACT	✓ Individual	✓ Team	✓ Group
PURPOSE	To examine self-perception and qualities of leadership		

DESCRIPTION

- Give one sheet of folded paper to each participant. Instruct the participants to open their sheets to form a 90 degree angle.

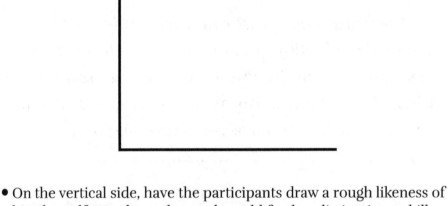

- On the vertical side, have the participants draw a rough likeness of him/herself. Words can be used to add further distinctions, skills, leadership capabilities, etc. After about five minutes, have them fold the paper over so the picture is at the back. Have each participant swap pictures with a trusted colleague.

- Instruct the colleague to draw a simple likeness of the other person and add the words which best describe that person's leadership skills.

- Once both halves of the paper are completed, have the two colleagues share the similarities and differences of each other's likeness and descriptive words.

DEBRIEF

? To what degree was there alignment between the two drawings?

? When alignment was not present, what transpired?

? How can better alignment be achieved?

MATERIALS

✓ One sheet of paper per participant, folded in half

SKILLSET	Creating Authenticity		
TOOL	Past — Present — Future		
IMPACT	Individual	✓ Team	✓ Group
PURPOSE	To identify characteristics of successful leaders		

DESCRIPTION

- Give participants three different colored index cards.

- On the first card (e.g., blue), ask the participants to identify someone from the past they have admired and respected. The admired person does not have to be identified. Ask the group members to think (silently and individually): "What was it about that person that made him/her successful?" Have them write 2–3 words or succinct phrases.

- On the second card (e.g., yellow) ask the participants to identify someone from their field (business, education, non-profit, sports, etc.) they admire and respect. The admired person does not have to be identified. Ask the group members to think (silently and individually): "What is it about that person that makes him/her successful?" Have them write 2–3 words or succinct phrases.

- Collect the two sets of cards. Select two sets of reporter/scribe teams and have them compile the information into two lists of PAST (blue cards) and PRESENT (yellow cards). Use chart paper posted at the front of the room. Ask scribes not to replicate the same words or ideas, but rather use slash marks.

- Once completed, ask participants to respond to their observations of the two lists. If discussion needs to be prompted, ask, "What type of characteristics are the majority of these words?" Trends? Comparison between charts? Note: Most often the words will describe attitudinal characteristics, not skills, knowledge, or experience.

- How did modeling these characteristics add to that particular person's success?

- After the debrief, have participants take the third card (e.g., pink) and write the 3–4 words that, if s/he embodies them, would help to make him/her successful. This "Future" card will not be collected, but rather the participants will take it back to their worksite to use as a reminder of what it takes to be successful.

DEBRIEF
? What must you do for others to recognize these qualities in you?

MATERIALS
✓ sets of 3 different colored notecards — 1 set per participant

✓ Chart paper

✓ Markers

ADAPTED FROM:
http://businessballs.com/freeteambuilddingactivities.htm

....

The key to successful leadership today is influence, not authority. ~ KENNETH BLANCHARD, AMERICAN AUTHOR AND MANAGEMENT CONSULTANT

....

SKILLSET	Creating Authenticity		
TOOL	Peanut Butter – Jelly Sandwich		
IMPACT	Individual	Team	✓ Group
PURPOSE	To demonstrate the importance of clear and complete communication		

DESCRIPTION

- Prepare index cards with the steps for making a peanut butter, jelly, and cracker sandwich as directed below — one step per card. In each set of cards, leave out one step. Prepare enough sets of cards for each team.

- Give each team a set of cards with small packets of peanut butter and jelly and crackers. Have teams make the "sandwich" per the exact instructions on the cards. Caution the groups to do only what is written on the cards. When a team encounters a missing step, they must stop.

- For each set of prepared cards (one set per team) remove a step — a different step for each team. There are 12 actual steps; give only 11 steps to each team. Do not number cards. For an additional challenge: shuffle each set prior to activity.

DEBRIEF

? What was missing in the completion of your task?

? What are some examples when incomplete instructions were given? What were the results?

MATERIALS

✓ Paper plates

✓ Knife per team

✓ Peanut butter – individual serving package – one per team

✓ Jelly packet – individual serving – one per team

✓ Saltine cracker package – individual serving (2 crackers per package)

✓ 3 × 5 cards on which each of the following steps is written (Do not number the cards.)

Open package of crackers

Take out one cracker

Set cracker on paper plate

Open package of peanut butter

Pick up knife

Scoop out peanut butter

Spread peanut butter on cracker

Open jelly packet

Squeeze jelly on top of peanut butter

Pick up knife

Put second cracker on top of jelly

Eat and enjoy

. . . .

The very essence of leadership is that you have to have a vision. It's got to be a vision you articulate clearly and forcefully on every occasion. You can't blow an uncertain trumpet. ~ REVEREND THEODORE M. HESBURGH, PRIEST AND PRESIDENT EMERITUS OF NOTRE DAME

. . . .

SKILLSET	Creating Authenticity		
TOOL	Press-Release		
IMPACT	Individual	✓ Team	✓ Group
PURPOSE	To brainstorm possible resolutions based on organizational concerns		

DESCRIPTION

- In small teams, have participants identify the "Pressing" issues/concerns of the the team or organization and write each one on a separate 3 × 5 card. Once issues/concerns are identified, give one per team.

- Using an enlarged copy of the chart provided, have the team brainstorm the constraints in one or more of the categories (Knowledge, Skill, Time, Money). After processing, have the team concisely filter through the ideas and identify 1–3 possible ideas to "release" the solution.

DEBRIEF

? Have each team prioritize issues and develop a possible timeline. Have each team report to total group.

Pressing Issue/ Concern	Constraints in the following areas				Releasing Possible Solutions
	Knowledge	Skills	Time	Money	

POSSIBLE EXTENSION

? Have teams identify the one (or more) person/position/team that would be the most appropriate to lead the solution.

MATERIALS

✓ One chart per team (may use poster or butcher paper)

✓ 3 × 5 note cards

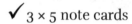

SKILLSET	Creating Authenticity		
TOOL	Trust — Low Trust		
IMPACT	Individual	✓ Team	✓ Group
PURPOSE	To demonstrate the reaction of individuals depending on their level of trust		

DESCRIPTION

- Prior to the training session, have a set of scenarios that are pertinent to the topic written on sheets of paper (e.g., present hardware does not have the needed memory; person responsible for tech support is on extended leave, etc.).

- After a workshop, training, or seminar focusing on a topic (for example, the implementation and roll out of a new computer software package), have the participants divide into groups of approximately 4–10 individuals.

- On a set of cards (one set per table) have the different roles written:

  - Supervisor - Trusting (one who has confidence in others)
  - Supervisor - Fluctuating Trust (one who vacillates between low trust and trust)
  - Supervisor - Low Trust (one who has little or no trust of others)
  - Employee - Trusting (one who has confidence in others)
  - Employee - Fluctuating Trust (one who vacillates between low trust and trust)
  - Employee - Low Trust (one who has little or no trust of others)

- Based on the role on the card selected, each person responds to the scenario. After a set time (approximately 15–20 minutes), have the group develop a set of characteristics displayed for Trusting, Fluctuating Trust, and Low Trust interactions.

- Groups can develop charts or verbally report to the total group.

DEBRIEF

? What can be done to develop a trusting environment in which the topic for the training session can be addressed?

MATERIALS

? Scenarios based on workshop topic

? Individual cards on which one of the roles and definition is written. Make sure there is a variety for each team.

- Supervisor - Trusting (one who has confidence in others)
- Supervisor - Fluctuating Trust (one who vacillates between low trust and trust)
- Supervisor - Low Trust (one who has little or no trust of others)
- Employee - Trusting (one who has confidence in others)
- Employee - Fluctuating Trust (one who vacillates between low trust and trust)
- Employee - Low Trust (one who has little or no trust of others)

. . . .

Even in traditional command—and—control environments, trust comes first and following comes second, not the other way around. Trust motivates people to go beyond mere compliance with authority. ~ JAMES KOUZES AND BARRY POSNER, AUTHORS OF *THE LEADERSHIP CHALLENGE*

. . . .

SKILLSET	Creating Authenticity		
TOOL	Balloon Board		
IMPACT	✓ Individual	✓ Team	✓ Group
PURPOSE	To model behavior that inspires trust		

DESCRIPTION

- Have one person (usually the leader of the team) stand on a board (large wooden board about 4 × 6 or 4 × 8). Have another board of the same size lying on the floor. This second board will actually have nails sticking up through the board (BE CAREFUL!!!). The nails will be all over the board usually in organized rows and columns (dozens of nails).

- Direct the attention of the participants to 2-3 dozen balloons that have been inflated and are just lying on the floor. Demonstrate that if any one balloon is placed on the board with nails that it would obviously pop.

- Put one balloon on the nail-board, and then place the board on which to stand on top of the board. The balloon would of course pop even easier.

- Take all of the balloons, space them across the nails and then cover the balloons with the other board. The team of balloons provides enough support to prevent one balloon from popping. In addition, one can even stand on the board and put weight on the balloons. The balloons will not pop.

- All of this is cool... but, the moment of trust comes into play when a few participants are asked to stand on the board with the facilitator. Even the weight of a few cannot pop all of the balloons because they have taken on all of the pressure together instead of singularly.

DEBRIEF

? What law of nature is demonstrated in this activity?

? How does the activity speak to the behavior in the organization?

? What are some of the parallels that can be drawn about "walking your talk"?

MATERIALS

✓ Two boards approximately 4' × 6' — one with no nails in it and the other with many nails in rows and columns.

✓ Balloons — about 30–50 — dependent upon size of board. Need enough balloons to be placed side-by-side over the total board

An activity similar to this can be found at: http://www.ehow.com/ how_7462762_explain-science-fair-experiment-project.html

....

Character makes trust possible, and trust is the foundation of leadership. ~ JOHN MAXWELL, EVANGELICAL PASTOR, AUTHOR AND SPEAKER

....

SKILLSET	Creating Authenticity		
TOOL	Now! How?		
IMPACT	Individual	✔ Team	✔ Group
PURPOSE	To analyze organizational concerns and brainstorm solutions		

DESCRIPTION

- Using a set of issues the organization is wrestling with, create charts (provided) with one issue written at the center of each chart. Place charts around the room. Give a marker to each participant.

- Have teams of 5–6 rotate every five minutes to each station and record what exists NOW! (what caused the issue, what was the catalyst, what were the conditions, etc.) and HOW? (what could be stopped, started, modified, realigned, etc.) to address the issue.

- Encourage participants to add new ideas or extensions of already cited ideas on the charts.

- After each team has been given time at each station (5–6 minutes), give one chart to each team to synthesize the information gathered and propose the most probable solution/s.

DEBRIEF
? Embedded in activity

MATERIALS
✔ Charts

✔ Markers

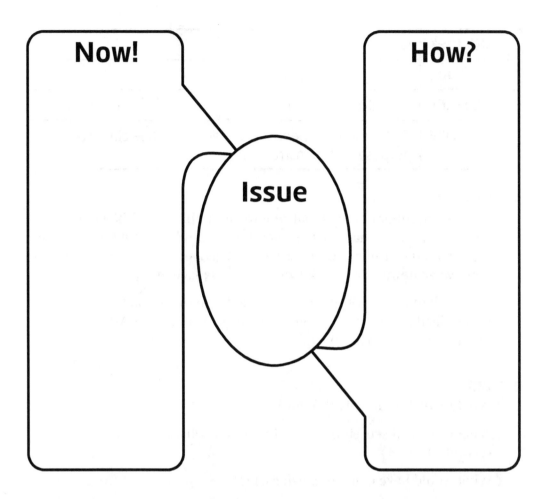

The ultimate measure of a man is not where he stands in moments of comfort, but where he stands at times of challenge and controversy. ~ MARTIN LUTHER KING, JR.

SKILLSET	Creating Authenticity		
TOOL	Putting It All Together		
IMPACT	Individual	✓ Team	✓ Group
PURPOSE	To illustrate the need for leaders to provide clarity of purpose and/or instructions		

DESCRIPTION

- Collect a number of items that require assembling by following directions, words, diagrams, or pictures. Examples might be a picture puzzle, model airplane kit, unassembled gadget, action figures, etc. Remove all items from the kit/box/etc. and place in Ziploc bags.

- Give each team one of the bags and ask them to complete the project. Do not lead the teams as to what the project should be. After about 10 minutes, stop the activity.

DEBRIEF

? What made this activity difficult?

? What was the discussion in your team as to what to do first, second, etc.?

? What would have made the task easier?

? What is the impact of instructions, or lack thereof?

? How would a model help?

? How does this relate to leadership?

MATERIALS

✓ picture puzzle – about a 200 piece puzzle (no box or photograph)

✓ model airplane kit – (no box or instruction sheet)

✓ unassembled gadget – (no instruction sheet) (dollar stores are a great source of such items)

✓ action figures – unassembled, removed from boxes

✓ Ziploc bags

....

There are three essentials to leadership: humility, clarity and courage. ~ FUCHAN YUAN, AUTHOR AND CHAN MASTER

....

SKILLSET	Creating Authenticity		
TOOL	Rainmakers		
IMPACT	Individual	✔ Team	✔ Group
PURPOSE	To demonstrate the role and impact of leaders		

DESCRIPTION

- Prior to the start of the activity, explain the different motions/actions and how the leader will randomly move through the group.

- Have participants sit so the leader can randomly move through the group. Have the leader begin the rainstorm by rubbing his/her hands together. The participants join in as the leader walks past them. (The leader may not pass by everyone with each change of action.)

- Instruct participants to continue with the activity demonstrated by the leader when he/she walks past. This swishing noise creates the sounds of soft rain. (Note: Some participants may be rubbing hands together throughout the whole activity.)

- Next, have the leader snap his/her fingers continuing to move randomly throughout the room. The participants continue to perform the previous action until the facilitator passes by them with a different motion. Other actions might include:

    - Clapping hands
    - Slapping thighs
    - Whistling wind
    - Etc.

- Finally, have the leader return to the rubbing of hands to "stop the rain."

DEBRIEF

? What was the impact of the leader on the group?

? What influenced decision-making?

? What was the response of participants when the leader did not come by them?

? How did the participants feel when "ignored"?

? How can these ideas be applied to actual dynamics in the organization?

MATERIALS
✓ None

SKILLSET	Creating Authenticity		
TOOL	What You See		
IMPACT	Individual	✓ Team	✓ Group
PURPOSE	To illustrate how physical characteristics/appearances can represent deeper leadership qualities		

DESCRIPTION

- Give each team a teddy bear (stuffed animal or paper cutout) along with "clothes" either real clothing or assorted colored paper on which participants can make the clothes.

- Instruct the teams to "dress" the teddy bear to represent a leader (not to be named — be careful if everyone is from the same company/ division). The clothes selected should represent the opinions of the group. On a sheet of paper, the team records the characteristics the clothes represent. Allow about 10 minutes.

- Have every two teams switch teddy bears. The receiving team records their observations about the teddy bear.

- After approximately 6–7 minutes, have the receiving team report their observations to the first team. Switch and have the other team give their report.

DEBRIEF

? What were the trends, similar comments, etc. as revealed in the team discussion?

? What are the characteristics that were observable?

? How do leaders become transparent?

? In what ways can leaders show transparency?

? Consider a personal reflection: What leadership characteristics do people see in me?

MATERIALS
✓ one teddy bear per team

✓ baby/children's clothing (second-hand stores have numerous items to use in this activity)

✓ If using paper teddy bears:

       ❧ paper/cardboard cutout of a bear
       ❧ sheets of paper with which to make clothes

SKILLSET	Creating Authenticity		
TOOL	Simon Says but Does		
IMPACT	Individual	✓ Team	✓ Group
PURPOSE	To consider the importance of leaders "walking their talk"		

DESCRIPTION

- Select 3–4 individuals to be "silent observers". The other team members or group members will be the participants. Remind the participants of the game "Simon Says". Most will have played it as children.

- Ask the observers to take notes about what they see — without talking to each other or giving other cues to the other observers or participants.

- Tell the participants that it is important to listen carefully to the instructions. Give several instructions in the traditional form of the game modeling what you say. After participants have warmed up, give an instruction such as "Simon says touch your right ear" but instead touch your right eye. Continue on with several more correct instructions and motions, followed by another instruction but different motion. Repeat as time allows and is effective. Give care not to over-extend the activity.

- Have observers report on insights (without identifying specific people). Have participants report on their reaction to an action different from the instruction given.

DEBRIEF

? Can an organization afford to have people off target?

? What happens when leaders purposefully mislead?

? What does misalignment look like to outside "observers"?

? How can these behaviors impact the effectiveness of the organization?

POSSIBLE EXTENSION

? Post the saying, "Do as I say, not as I do." Have participants break into groups of 2–4 to discuss the statement.

MATERIALS
✓ None

SKILLSET	Creating Authenticity		
TOOL	Profile Puzzle		
IMPACT	✔ Individual	✔ Team	✔ Group
PURPOSE	To identify the characteristics of an authentic person		

DESCRIPTION

- Choose a leader from history, the present, in the community, or organization.

- Draw a rectangle as the puzzle boarder and a "puzzle piece" (within the rectangle) on a large sheet of butcher paper. Place the name of the chosen person on the first puzzle piece.

- Have participants draw additional puzzle pieces adjoining the first one and place in each puzzle piece one word that describes an attribute or characteristic that person possesses which creates/created authenticity: genuineness, transparency, truthfulness, etc.

- Encourage participants to draw additional puzzle pieces until the total puzzle is completed.

DEBRIEF

? Do these words clearly define the person identified?

? What evidence (activities, interactions, incidents, etc.) supports the word choice?

? How does this person's attributes challenge you to a higher level of authenticity?

MATERIALS

✔ Butcher paper

✔ Markers

✔ If done as a small team or individually, rather than butcher paper, use chart paper or an 8½" × 11" sheet of paper.

Note: To reduce the time needed, the puzzle pieces can be drawn prior to the session.

ANCHORS

· · · · · · · · · · · · · · · · · · · ·

As an authentic organizational leader, you must acknowledge your personal strengths, weaknesses, beliefs, and passions. You must choose high ethical standards and practices for yourself and your organization and communicate these as standards expected of all people who work in the organization.

Recognized as leading authorities on the subject of authentic leadership, George, Sims, and Gergen (2007), in their work entitled *True North: Discover Your Authentic Leadership*, wrote:

> Authentic leaders are genuine people who are true to themselves and what they believe. Rather than letting the expectations of others guide them, they are prepared to be their own person and go their own way. As they develop as authentic leaders, they are more concerned about serving others than they are about their own success or recognition. And they are constantly looking for ways to grow personally. Authentic leaders develop genuine connections with others and engender trust. Because people trust them, they are able to motivate people to high levels of performance by empowering them to lead. (p. 206)

To build a community of authenticity, Hyatt (2012), in an article entitled "The Five Marks of Authentic Leadership," identified five qualities for leaders:

1. Having insight,

2. Demonstrating initiative,

3. Exerting influence,

4. Having impact, and

5. Exercising integrity.

To be a truly authentic leader, you must intentionally integrate all five of these qualities. The absence of any one quality undermines your leadership.

People in your organization have the right to expect leaders to have a level of competence — knowledge and skills — that demonstrates an understanding of the organization, its structure, capabilities, direction, resources, and people. In Spears' (1995) *Reflections on Leadership*, Tarr quotes Tom Peters in referring to competence of organizations. Peters identified three distinctive areas of competency in excellent organizations:

1. They have superior customer service;

2. They have internal entrepreneurship;

3. They have a 'bone-deep' belief in the dignity, worth, and creative potential of every person in the organization" (p. 83).

It follows, therefore, that to lead excellent organizations competently, you must exhibit commitment to others; take the risk to build a creative, innovative enterprise, and demonstrate that they believe in the value of all stakeholders involved in the organization. Cox and Hoover (1992) stated, "An organization will never rise above the quality of its leadership" (p. 39).

To lead effectively, competence is essential, but competence alone is inadequate. Another essential leadership quality is character. A person's character is an outgrowth of values and choices. Lowney (2003) wrote, "Leadership is a way of living in which basic life strategies and principles reinforce one another" (p. 245).

> *Courage is the enforcing virtue, the one that makes possible all the other virtues common to exceptional leaders: honesty, integrity, confidence, compassion and humility.*
>
> ~JOHN MCCAIN,
> U.S. SENATOR

Authenticity is the degree to which you are true to your own personality, spirit, and character despite the pressures — owning your own personal experiences (values, thoughts, emotions, and beliefs) and acting in accordance to your true self (expressing what you really think and believe and behaving accordingly.) In an article on authentic and servant leadership, Nayab (2013) suggested that leaders who are authentic are driven by character; they develop personality and character intentionally through learning, experiencing, observing, and reflecting. The choice of values and the resulting actions taken determine in large part whether or not a leader is effective or ineffective.

In a similar vein, Irwin (2009) asserted that

We always become who we are. It may take time or stress or illness, but what's inside of us tends to come out. Our character serves as the wellspring from which our behavior emerges. Just as Os Guiness said: 'Character....is the essential "stuff" a person is made of, the inner reality and quality in which thought, speech, decision, behavior and relations are rooted.' As such, character determines behavior just as behavior demonstrates character." (p. 100–101)

> *Example is not the main thing in influencing others, it is the only thing.*
> ~ ALBERT SCHWEITZER, GERMAN THEOLOGIAN, PHYSICIAN, AND MEDICAL MISSIONARY

George et. al. (2007) stated, "Authentic leaders demonstrate a passion for their purpose, practice their values consistently, lead with their hearts as well as their heads. They establish long-term meaningful relationships and have the self-discipline to get results. They know who they are. (p. 205)

Trust by coworkers is essential to your effectiveness as a leader. Stephen M.R. Covey (2006) asserted that "Trust is equal parts character and competence. Both are absolutely necessary. From the family room to the board room, you can look at any leadership failure and it is always a failure of one or the other" (pp. 30–31). Further, he said that "in order to create transparency, among other things, leaders must tell the truth; get real (What you see is what you get.); be open and authentic; reveal information and err on the side of disclosure" (p. 157).

Along with competence and character, you must possess compassion to be known as an authentic leader. Shipka (1997) defined compassion in the following way: "Compassion is being fully present, really listening to and being with another person. Through such a presence, you are being given the possibility of clearly seeing into the soul of another" (p. 126).

In *The Truth about Leadership*, Kouzes and Posner (2010) quoted educator Parker Palmer who insisted that "The power of authentic leadership ... is found not only in external arrangements but in the human heart. Authentic leaders in every setting — from families to nation states — aim at liberating the heart, their own and others, so that its power can liberate the world." (2006). Kouzes and Posner explained that "Nothing external is going to save us — not government, not companies, not technology nor heroes on white horses. But imagine what can be done when people experience the power of the human heart" (p. 136).

You should not mistake compassion for a soft approach that allows people to shirk their responsibilities. Compassion involves empathy, concern, and caring for others, helping them to be successful while at the same time holding them accountable. Palmer (2008) suggested that having compassion is helping people to reclaim their soul deep identity. *Passion* comes from the Latin for suffering. *Com* is a prefix meaning *with*; thus, according to Kouzes and Posner (2006) in *A Leader's Legacy,*

> A compassionate person is someone who suffers with and shares the suffering of others and wants to take action to alleviate this condition. Nearly every act of leadership requires suffering and, often for the leader, a choice between one's personal success and safety and the greater welfare of others (p. 5).

Advocating the importance of helping people to be their "true and best," Parrott (2006) expressed that "Inner strength is the energy that supports healthy relationships, good character, mature wisdom and purpose in life" (pp. 13, 17–18).

Hasselbein and Goldsmith (2006) discussed a balance between compassion and courage:

> *Good management is largely a matter of love. Or if you're uncomfortable with that word call it caring, because proper management involves caring for people, not manipulating them.*
>
> ~ JAMES AUTRY, FORMER FORTUNE 500 EXECUTIVE AND AUTHOR OF *THE SERVANT LEADER*

> I combine these two attributes into one because they work best together. In concert, courage and compassion call for the ability to act decisively and strategically while maintaining a reverence for life. The union of courage and compassion enables us to bravely see problems as opportunities, to hear complaints as different (and potentially valuable) ideas and perspectives, to understand resistance as possibility, and to boldly recognize that most people in our lives are doing the best they can with who they are and what they know. (p. 300)

They suggested that compassion and courage are intertwined giving credence to love being the source of a leader's courage. Fairholm (2000) discussed this concept extensively throughout *Capturing the Heart of Leadership: Spirituality and Community in the New American Workplace.*

Bennis (1989) equated courage with integrity when he said, "By integrity, I mean standards of moral and intellectual honesty on which our conduct is based. Without integrity, we betray ourselves and others and cheapen every endeavor" (p. 117). And in *Moral Intelligence*, Lennick and Kiel (2008) succinctly identified the substance of the matter saying "Integrity is authenticity" (p. 80).

Emphasizing the importance of courage, Irwin (2009) stated,

> Courage emanates from our resolute beliefs and core convictions .... Absent any real beliefs and convictions and the courage that rests on them, we become tentative, or worse, expedient. We then want to just get along and line up with the prevailing opinion ... Courage is not being unafraid. It's about choosing to do the right thing under difficult circumstances. Courageous individuals are people not caught up in their own importance or presuming that they are somehow more important or virtuous or impervious than others. (p. 149–150)

> *It requires vision, initiative, patience, respect, persistence, courage, and faith to be a transforming leader.*
>
> ~STEPHEN R. COVEY, AMERICAN EDUCATOR, AUTHOR, BUSINESSMAN, AND SPEAKER

Fred Smith, CEO of FedEx, underscored an important related point, "People with humility don't deny their power; they just recognize that it passes through them, not from them" (Blanchard, 2010, p. 276).

In his groundbreaking work *The Fifth Discipline*, Senge (2006) defined building community more specifically as creating a 'learning community' or 'learning organization'. Emphasizing the importance of this as a foundation for an effective organization, he identified four disciplines that are required to create a learning community: Personal Mastery, Mental Models, Shared Vision, and Team Learning. Combined, these disciplines create the fifth discipline known as Systems Thinking, the discipline that results in coordinated organizational effectiveness. To successfully create a 'learning community' requires intentional and consistent attention. And, it takes a courageous leader to guide the organization through these disciplines.

Underscoring the importance of authenticity, George, Sims, and Gergen (2007) identified five dimensions of authentic leaders. The qualities they cited are:

- "Understanding their purpose
- Practicing solid values
- Leading with heart
- Establishing connected relationships
- Demonstrating self-discipline" (p. 11).

This section emphasizes the priority that you as a leader must give to creating a community that is characterized by trust and authenticity. Only through authentic leadership in a trusting environment can you build true community.

. . . .

The supreme quality of leadership is integrity.
~ DWIGHT EISENHOWER, 34TH AMERICAN PRESIDENT

. . . .

Delegating to Strengths

HOW DO YOU EMPOWER OTHERS?

The sailors' hats signify individuals who have committed their skills and availability to the organization. An effective captain delegates both responsibility and authority to appropriate shipmates.

The most important duty of the captain is to assemble a competent crew that has the necessary skills, abilities, and attitudes to perform required responsibilities as well as the potential for continuous development. The captain cannot stand at the wheel all, or even most, of the time. Trustworthy shipmates are needed to whom responsibility can be delegated. They must have the skill to employ available navigational tools and periodically be guided by the directional beacons from the lighthouse. Identifying specific strengths, training, and personal interests of each crew member informs the captain's decisions about delegating opportunities that allow each crew member to own assigned tasks, to make decisions, and to be accountable for the outcomes.

To fulfill the purpose of any organization, it is vital to have competent workers in appropriate job functions. A challenge of delegation is striking a balance between control and empowerment. Leaders must give up control of the process but hold the worker accountable for results. If done well, a "leaderful" organization, as described by Raelin, (2003) will develop.

TOOLS FOR DELEGATING TO STRENGTHS

SKILLSET	Delegating to Strengths		
TOOL	Sitting on the Bus		
IMPACT	✓ Individual	Team	Group
PURPOSE	To identify the right people for specific jobs		

DESCRIPTION

- Have participant develop a chart with the bird's eye view of a bus (Provided.)

- Put in the number of seats for each of the positions within the department, team, etc. for whom the leader is responsible. Using note cards, write the job description/responsibilities for each position within the department, team, etc. Place these notecards – one per seat.

- Using a different color set of note cards, write the names of each person in the department, team, etc. Under the name of the person, write his/her strengths, talents, skills, and specialized training, certification, or education.

- Without regard for who is presently assigned to a given job/ responsibility, place the person with the specific skill set on the seat most closely matching the job description. If more than one person matches a given job, place each of their cards on that seat.

- Examine the chart. Look for empty seats, multiple people in seats, etc.

DEBRIEF

? What does the configuration of cards indicate?

? Are there too many employees with the same skill set?

? Are there not enough employees with the needed skills?

? Are there totally empty seats?

? How will this information inform hiring practices?

? Are there possibilities to move people within the department?

? Are there some cards that were not placed on any seat? What might be the implications? Are there possibilities of movement to a different department/team?

MATERIALS

✓ 3 × 5 note cards (two different colors) enough for every position and person in the department/team

✓ Chart of bus – may be best prepared on poster board

Note: This activity should occur in private with only the leader or the leader and a facilitator. The activity and the information from the processing of the activity should not be common knowledge unless there is a trusting environment and everyone is in consensus with the information.

THIS ACTIVITY IS BASED ON

Collins, J. (2001). *Good to Great: Why some companies make the leap...and others don't.* New York City: Harper Business.

....

The secret of success is not in doing your own work but in recognizing the right man [person] to do it.~ ANDREW CARNEGIE

....

SKILLSET	Delegating to Strengths
TOOL	The Waste Can
IMPACT	✓ Individual ✓ Team ✓ Group
PURPOSE	To help empower individuals by identifying the alignment between their job and their personal skill set

DESCRIPTION

- Have participants sit in a circle. Place a waste can in the center of the circle.

- On a blue card, have each participant identify the skill, knowledge, and experiences needed for his/her specific job for which they were hired.

- On a yellow card, have each participant identify two projects or assignments they are currently doing or that are upcoming.

- Have all participants fold the cards in half.

- Collect all cards (blue and yellow) in the waste can.

- After all have been collected, stir cards until well mixed.

- Move around the circle with the waste can asking the participants to pull both a blue card and a yellow card.

- Group participants into pairs (preferably those not working together on a daily basis or good friends) and process the information on the two cards. Encourage the pairs to look for alignment between the two cards and how suited the assignments on the yellow card are to the skills, knowledge, and experiences of the blue card.

- Discuss the "waste" that "can" result from misalignment of skills with job function.

DEBRIEF

? What might be the personal feeling when there is an obvious lack of alignment?

? What might a person do if there was better alignment with his/her personal skill set and his/her job assignments?

? How does this relate to the job site? (Caution participants, especially if they are familiar with each other's place of work, that this is not a time to reference particular people or situations.)

MATERIALS

✓ Blue and yellow 4 × 6 note cards – one per participant (may use different colors)

✓ Waste can

. . . .

The single biggest way to impact an organization is to focus on leadership development. There is almost no limit to the potential of an organization that recruits good people, raises them up as leaders and continually develops them.

~ JOHN C. MAXWELL, EVANGELICAL PASTOR, AUTHOR AND SPEAKER

. . . .

SKILLSET	Delegating to Strengths		
TOOL	Dance, Dance, Dance		
IMPACT	✓ Individual	✓ Team	✓ Group
PURPOSE	To emphasize the value of people and empower them to see, build upon, and begin to write their legacy		

DESCRIPTION

- Distribute a copy of the poem "The Dash" to each participant provided.

- Have participants silently read the poem. Show the video of "The Dash" from the internet site: www.simpletruths.com

- Ask participants to think about their own dance across the dash and to reflect on the questions as they are read aloud:

    - How would your dance look?
    - What music would be playing during your dance?
    - Who would be there to dance with you?
    - To whom would you dedicate your dance across the dash?
    - How will your dance across the dash positively influence or contribute to the dash of others?

- Provide each participant with a 5-inch cardstock circle to represent a CD (compact disc). Ask each participant to record the following information on their circle:

    - The name of the dance
    - The name of the song for the dance
    - A written dedication

(Note: Play "I Hope You Dance," or another appropriate song, as background music as the participants complete their circles.)

DEBRIEF

? How did the image of a "dash" impact your thinking about your life?

? What are the ways you can use this information?

MATERIALS

- Card stock circle cutouts (CDs) – one per participant

- Poem – The Dash http://lindaellis.net/the-dash/the-dash-poem-by-linda-ellis/
- Music: *I Hope You Dance* by Lee Ann Womack, or another appropriate song

....

It is always worthwhile to make others aware of their worth. ~MALCOLM FORBES, PUBLISHER, FORBES MAGAZINE

....

SKILLSET	Delegating to Strengths		
TOOL	Resident Experts		
IMPACT	✔ Individual	✔ Team	✔ Group
PURPOSE	To empower members to acknowledge and use the talents of others		

DESCRIPTION

- Create a large chart (sample provided) on which each person's name in the department or team is posted. In the row beside their name, each person lists his/her skills, trainings, hobbies, education, certifications, etc.

- Other people can also add additional skills, talents, etc. to other people's lists.

- Post the chart in a workspace specifically for employees (lounge, workroom, etc).

- Encourage the participants to use this information to identify people who have the skills needed for a given project.

- Continue the chart to include a row per person in the department or team.

Name	Skills	Trainings	Certifications	Talents	Hobbies

DEBRIEF

? How can this information be used to empower a person? The team?

? What are some possible situations in which someone would use this information?

MATERIALS

✓ Chart (butcher paper, poster board, etc.)

✓ Markers

....

As we look ahead into the next century, leaders will be those who empower others. ~ BILL GATES, AMERICAN BUSINESS MAGNATE AND PHILANTHROPIST

....

SKILLSET	Delegating to Strengths		
TOOL	Egg-Cellent Passion		
IMPACT	Individual	✓ Team	✓ Group
PURPOSE	To focus talent on results, not methods		

DESCRIPTION

- Distribute a set of materials as listed below to each team of 3–5 members. Announce that the objective is to create a way to safely get the egg to roll from the top of the table and onto the ground — without breaking. The egg must roll freely. No one can touch the egg or the support mechanism designed by the team once the egg has been released.

- Roam from team to team and give help ONLY if requested. (If a team asks for other resources, provide them within reason.)

- Encourage all teams to complete the task; acknowledge the team that completes the task first.

DEBRIEF

? How did your team go about planning for the construction? Did everyone agree? If not, what happened?

? Were there members of the team who chose not to participate? What happened?

? Was there one individual who took over the activity?

? Did anyone ask for help or additional materials? If not, why not?

? If your team was unsuccessful, what transpired?

? If your team was successful, what happened to cause it?

MATERIALS

✓ Per each team:

> Scissors
>
> Large piece of cloth
>
> One uncooked egg
>
> File folders
>
> Tape
>
> Straws

✓ Cleaning supplies

....

Few things help an individual more than to place responsibility upon them and to let them know that you trust them. ~ BOOKER T. WASHINGTON, AFRICAN-AMERICAN EDUCATOR AND ADVISOR TO U. S. PRESIDENTS

....

SKILLSET	Delegating to Strengths		
TOOL	2 Questions — 3 Responses		
IMPACT	Individual	✓ Team	✓ Group
PURPOSE	To quickly identify strengths and passions of employees		

DESCRIPTION

- Pass out one 4 × 6 card to each participant. Ask the participants to respond to the following:

  - On the front of the card, place your name and your response to this question:
    "If I were to have a conversation with the CEO, Director, Boss, etc. of the company at which you work and your name came up in the discussion, what three things would you want me to tell him/her about you?"
  - On the back of the card, ask participants to respond to this question:
    "If you had a magic wand, what three things would you change about this business (church, company, school, department, etc.)?"

- Thank the participants for the information, collect the cards, and move on to other activities.

DEBRIEF

Note: the information collected from each employee can assist the leader when needing to delegate to strengths.

? The first question (three things to tell someone about the employee) will assist the leader in knowing what that employee wants to be known for. This will allow the leader to find opportunities to reinforce these things. For example, the employee wants to be known for being an innovative team player, as a leader look for occasions where that person can serve in that role.

? The second question (three things you would change) will assist the leader in knowing the areas of employee's passion. For example, if a person indicates that they would like to change the way software is so frequently altered, when the next opportunity for software selection or update occurs, ask that person to serve on the team making the decisions.

MATERIALS
✓ 4 × 6 cards – one per person

....

Treat people as though they were what they ought to be and you will help them become what they are capable of being.

~ JOHANN WOLFGANG VON GOETHE, GERMAN WRITER AND POLITICIAN

....

SKILLSET	Delegating to Strengths		
TOOL	What is it?		
IMPACT	Individual	✓ Team	✓ Group
PURPOSE	To illustrate the impact of empowerment in problem solving		

DIRECTIONS

- Divide participants into two or more groups (depending on size of groups). Give each group a box of supplies. Each group will have the same supplies. On slips of paper, write the following: train, skyscraper, bridge, sailboat, waterfall, bus, helicopter, castle.

- Fold the paper strips. Have one member from each group pull out one slip and tell the members of the group the object written on the paper.

- Groups use only the supplies in the box to create the object. The only rule is that all participants must have an active role in creating the object. Walk from group to group, choose one or two groups to interrupt and tell them they are doing it wrong and need to do it differently. Nod and smile or compliment the other groups. Give the groups enough time to complete the object, approximately 15–20 minutes.

- Allow time for groups to view each other's masterpieces.

DEBRIEF

? What was the impact of the facilitator's approval (or disapproval) statements on the project?

? How did the facilitator's interruptions impact the team?

? What challenges developed among the team members?

? Did individual team members demonstrate strengths or skills?

? Did all team members respond in the same way to the facilitator's interactions?

MATERIALS

✔ Box of supplies for each group:

       Paper clips

       Drinking Straws

       Masking Tape

       Plastic milk jugs

       10 pieces of construction paper

       Wax paper

✔ Additional items – equal in each box.

....

The only way to make a man trustworthy
is to trust him. ~ ANONYMOUS

....

SKILLSET	Delegating to Strengths		
TOOL	Affirmation Wall		
IMPACT	Individual	✓ Team	✓ Group
PURPOSE	To encourage individuals and teams to use their strengths		

DESCRIPTION

- Put a large piece of butcher paper (or similar material) on a large wall or bulletin board. Draw a large rectangle on the paper and divide the chart according to the number of teams in the department.

- Encourage team members to write descriptors about each of the other teams. Descriptors may include words like: cooperative, insightful, innovative, skilled, etc. (This can be an ongoing activity.)

- As the specific teams work throughout the year on different projects and activities when they demonstrate one of the descriptors, that team encircles the word. If that descriptor is demonstrated the second time, the team draws another circle around the word.

DEBRIEF

Note: Periodically, in an employee meeting or department meeting, the leader may refer to the board and specifics on it.

? At the close of a quarter, or some specific time, debrief with the department:

? How did other descriptors empower your team?

? What impact did the action of encircling a descriptor have on your team?

? How did the public display of this information impact the team?

MATERIALS

✓ Large wall space or bulletin board

✓ Butcher paper or similar material

✓ Markers

· ·

There is something that is much more scarce, something rarer than ability. It is the ability to recognize ability.

~ ROBERT HALF, AMERICAN HUMAN RESOURCE FIRM

· ·

SKILLSET	Delegating to Strengths		
TOOL	Seven Cs		
IMPACT	Individual	✓ Team	✓ Group
PURPOSE	To help individuals see the similarities and differences between people		

DESCRIPTION

- Give each participant a copy of the form (provided). Have each person select another person to talk with to identify 7 things they have in Common and 7 things that are Not Common

- After approximately 3–4 minutes, have the members switch partners and repeat the process.

- Do this the third time.

DEBRIEF

? What did you find out?

? What did you find interesting?

? How can you use this information?

? How will this information impact your relationships?

? How can this information assist you as you work together?

MATERIALS

✓ Worksheet – one per participant

SEVEN Cs

. . . .

Partner:	Partner:	Partner:
_____	_____	_____
Common	Common	Common
1_____	1_____	1_____
2_____	2_____	2_____
3_____	3_____	3_____
4_____	4_____	4_____
5_____	5_____	5_____
6_____	6_____	6_____
7_____	7_____	7_____
Not Common	Not Common	Not Common
1_____	1_____	1_____
2_____	2_____	2_____
3_____	3_____	3_____
4_____	4_____	4_____
5_____	5_____	5_____
6_____	6_____	6_____
7_____	7_____	7_____

SKILLSET	Delegating to Strengths		
TOOL	ZPAC		
IMPACT	Individual	✓ Team	✓ Group
PURPOSE	To explore four attributes of empowered teams		

DESCRIPTION

- Divide group into four teams. Give a printed copy of the team instructions (provided) along with one of the following words: Zealous, Pliable, Adaptable, and Courageous.

- Using the assigned word, have the team read the instructions in full, identify the roles, and complete the activity. Each team is given chart paper and markers.

- Allow 20–30 minutes for teamwork.

- Have teams display their work and give an oral presentation.

DEBRIEF

? What was the challenge in creating the story?

? How did the team work to accomplish the task?

? What was the process by which roles were assigned?

? Did the assignments match specific skills?

? What was the level of involvement dependent upon autonomy?

? What is the importance of the four words to team effectiveness?

MATERIALS/PRIOR PREPARATION

✓ Chart paper

✓ Markers

✓ Words written on cardstock: Zealous, Pliable, Adaptable, Courageous

✓ Instruction sheets

TEAM INSTRUCTIONS

Use the assigned word (Zealous, Pliable, Adaptable, or Courageous) as a theme to create a story.

Time: 20–30 minutes

Assign each member of the team to serve in one of the following roles:

- **Coordinator:** Coordinates the entire team! S/He will introduce the members of the team and the role that each played in this assignment.

- **Recorder:** Records all the information supplied by team members onto a chart.

- **Lexicographer:** Creates the definition of assigned word, including its root derivative. (No dictionaries allowed – electronic or otherwise.) S/He will also direct the attention of the audience to the chart when information is shared.

- **Graphic Artist:** Creates a graphic illustration or logo that best depicts the meaning of the assigned word.

- **Famous Authors** (1 or more): Work together to create a story that describes the assigned word. The story must begin with "Once upon a time...." and conclude with "The End. Only two characters can be used in the story.

- **Balladeer:** Reads the story to the entire group – enthusiastically!

SKILLSET	Delegating to Strengths		
TOOL	Design Me		
IMPACT	Individual	✓ Team	✓ Group
PURPOSE	To have individuals identify his/her attributes		

DESCRIPTION

- Give each group a set of sample wallpaper sheets – the more colorful, bold, designed paper, the better. Allow participants to select one.

- Give each participant an 8½ × 11 sheet of plain paper. Have participants fold the blank sheet in half.

- Using the selected wallpaper sample, have each participant identify descriptors of the sample. Write the descriptors on the left side of the sheet of paper provided. Allow about 3–4 minutes. On the right half, have the participants identify their personal strengths. Allow 3–4 minutes.

- Have each participant compare the two columns – have him/her identify the common descriptors and those that are not the same.

- Have the participants at a table discuss their findings.

DEBRIEF

? What observations did your team members see?

? What was the parallel between the attributes of the wallpaper and their personal attributes?

? How can this information be used in a team setting?

MATERIALS

✓ Sample wallpaper books

✓ Plain 8 ½" × 11" paper — folded in half

Wallpaper	Self

SKILLSET	Delegating to Strengths		
TOOL	Come Together		
IMPACT	Individual	✓ Team	✓ Group
PURPOSE	To match skills to job tasks		

DESCRIPTION

- Divide participants into four or five teams. Give each participant a notecard with a career/job written on it. Hand these out at random.

- Ask the participants to use the back of the card to list the skills, knowledge, and personal attributes needed to best fulfill that job.

- Give each team a scenario that is generic or specific to their type of business (see sample below). Have the teams problem-solve the scenario considering the information on the cards.

- Allow 5–7 minutes for discussion.

DEBRIEF

✓ How was your team able to problem-solve using the different people involved?

✓ Were there any skills not represented? What did your team do to compensate?

✓ Did the best person for the particular areas of the scenario step up to offer their skills?

MATERIALS

✓ Prior to activity, develop scenarios that are related to the organization — one per group/team

✓ 4 × 6 cards with job/careers written on them:

        Coach

        Religious Leader

        CEO

        Custodian

        Teacher

Salesman

Researcher

Engineer

✓ ...and any others depending upon configuration of group

SAMPLE SCENARIO:

....

A new program, as required by a newly passed state regulation, is to be in operation in six months. This will cost the organization approximately 10% of the total income in training, time away from job responsibilities, and loss of products, thus impacting the budget's bottom line.

....

Leaders don't create followers, they create more leaders. ~ TOM PETERS, AUTHOR, *IN SEARCH OF EXCELLENCE*

....

SKILLSET	Delegating to Strengths		
TOOL	Where Am I?		
IMPACT	✓ Individual	✓ Team	✓ Group
PURPOSE	To empower individuals to identify specific needs and support		

DESCRIPTION

- Based on *Situational Leadership* by Blanchard and Hersey (1988), give each participant a copy of the Situational Leadership worksheet. Explain the quadrants as delineated by Blanchard and Hersey.

- Identify a list of tasks/projects specific to the organization or business such as: leading a new project, overseeing a group activity, reviewing data reports, working with the board of directors, maintaining detailed records, preparing marketing materials, etc.

- For each task/project have participants individually identify in which quadrant they perceive they are and what support, if any, they will need from their supervisor. It will be important for employees to understand that everyone is in different quadrants at different times for different tasks. Have participants use the worksheet to identify their status for each project/activity. Reproduce worksheets as needed or place two or more on one sheet with specific projects or tasks identified.

- Collect individual charts or schedule meetings to discuss information.

Note: This can only be effectively done in a trusting environment. Employees must be confident that this information will not be punitive.

DEBRIEF
? Personal conversations

MATERIALS
✓ Individual chart for each participant (provided)

Project/Task:	
have some skills not very excited about the task	have low skills very excited about the task
have high skill sets excited about task	have low skills not interested in task

Project/Task:	
have some skills not very excited about the task	have low skills very excited about the task
have high skill sets excited about task	have low skills not interested in task

Project/Task:	
have some skills not very excited about the task	have low skills very excited about the task
have high skill sets excited about task	have low skills not interested in task

SKILLSET	Delegating to Strengths		
TOOL	Puzzled Thumbs		
IMPACT	Individual	✓ Team	✓ Group
PURPOSE	To experience the limitations in accomplishing a task		

DIRECTIONS

- Divide the participants into teams of 3-5 people. Give each team a puzzle of approximately 75–100 pieces. Have teams separate all the pieces and place them face-up on the table so that no puzzle pieces are touching any other piece.

- Time the teams as they assemble their puzzles.

- Stop the teams when they are about half finished with the puzzles. Hand out pieces of masking tape. Have each team member tape his/her thumbs to their hands so that they are no longer able to be used.

- Have the teams continue to assemble the puzzle.

DEBRIEF

? What was the difference between both halves of the activity?

? Was your team able to keep the momentum during the second half?

? How does this relate to your specific worksite?

? How did it feel when a vital tool (thumb) was removed from your use – without your permission?

MATERIALS

✓ Children's puzzles – approximately 75–100 pieces

✓ Masking tape

Read more at http://www.brainyquote.com/quotes/keywords/teamwork. html#cDA6GyEWF3VVZ6YD.99

. . . .

Unity is strength... when there is teamwork and collaboration, wonderful things can be achieved. ~ MATTIE STEPANEK

. . . .

SKILLSET	Delegating to Strengths		
TOOL	Hire Me? Just ASK!		
IMPACT	✔ Individual	✔ Team	✔ Group
PURPOSE	To have individuals assess the alignment of their strengths to their job placement		

DIRECTIONS

- Give each participant the ASK! Form (provided). Have participants identify the major attitudes (dispositions), skills, and knowledge needed for their jobs.

- Once participants have completed the list, have them develop interview questions they would ask an applicant seeking a similar position.

- Without any discussion, have participants reflect on the questions, their personal responses to the questions, and whether or not they would hire themselves.

- With a trusted colleague, have the participants debrief their personal reflections.

DEBRIEF

? Was there an attribute that was difficult to identify?

? How did you personally respond to the fact that you may not be the best fit for your present position?

? How can this information be used in the organization? In personal careers?

MATERIALS

✔ ASK form – one per participant

Read more at http://www.brainyquote.com/quotes/keywords/win. html#3dp33crQQw2mvolf.99

ASK! Attitudes, Skills, Knowledge

. . . .

Identify the top 5–6 Attitudes (Dispositions), Skills, and Knowledge needed for your present job. Try to identify at least one in each area (attitude, skill, and knowledge). Put each one in the ( ) beside the numerals.

1.(_____)

_____

_____

2.(_____)

_____

_____

3.(_____)

_____

_____

4.(_____)

_____

_____

5.(_____)

_____

_____

6.(_____)

_____

_____

7.(_____)

_____

_____

ANCHORS

· · · · · · · · · · · · · · · · · · ·

To be an effective organizational leader, you must learn to delegate appropriately to your co-workers. To delegate well, you must know the strengths, weaknesses, preferences and ambitions of your workers and know the tasks and roles needed by the organization. It is important that you understand that you cannot "do it all" alone.

Leadership coach and facilitator, Megan Tough (2013) emphasized in *Delegate or Die*, that:

> There is not a single management skill more critical to your personal and professional success as an entrepreneur than learning to delegate. But delegating successfully is much more than simply handing out assignments. It is more an exercise in understanding and accepting our own strengths and limitations....In this fast paced world, we must choose what activities it makes sense for us to do ourselves, and what it makes sense to let go of. None of us can be an expert in everything - not because of any lack of intellectual ability, but more because we lack specific exposure or experience. We must learn to accept this fact and be OK with it. (Paras 1 & 2)

Baldoni (2005) stated, "Empowerment begins with the belief in yourself and a willingness to give something of yourself so that others can participate in the endeavor" (p. 106). He listed five ways to make empowerment a reality in the workplace:

1. identify the opportunity,

2. give responsibility,

3. distribute authority,

4. hold people accountable, and

5. empower others.

In their landmark study *Situational Leadership,* Blanchard and Hersey (1988) identified four levels of interactions that leaders may have with their subordinates when delegating assignments: directing, coaching, supporting, and delegating. The leader must know the commitment and ability of the employee to identify which level of interaction is appropriate. The degree of the employee's need for emotional support and instruction determines the amount (level or style) of oversight needed from the leader. Reh (2013) warned "Delegate...Don't Just Dump" (about.com). Leaders must avoid the temptation to dump activities and responsibilities that they do not prefer to do themselves. Delegation should achieve two purposes: lighten the leader's load and help the receiver learn and grow.

Recognizing the importance of delegating based on strengths, Henman (2010) asserted:

> The keynote of success is managing strengths, not attempting to mitigate weaknesses. No individual or organization has ever achieved excellence through corrective action. Only by recognizing talent and working to develop it can you hope to succeed in your own life and to positively influence the professional growth of others. (Para.1)

Numerous tools are available to assist you working together with your employees in assessing strengths. Prominent tools include:

Clifton & Buckingham's Strengthfinders, (www.strength-finders.com);

Myers-Briggs Personality Inventory (http://www.myersbriggs.org/my-mbti-personality-type/mbti-basics/); and

DISC (www.onlinediscprofile.com/).

A case study from Business and Legal Reports Inc. (2008) reported that "the Ritz Carlton difference starts with employee recruitment and hiring" (p.3). The process includes interviews that result in a behavior profile that shows if the applicant has characteristics high in empathy, inquisitiveness, and interest in customer service. Employees are empowered to solve problems and make decisions that result in extraordinary customer service. Managers receive additional help developing their roles in mentoring and coaching within the organization. The emphasis is on developing the employee's ability to use his/her own intellect, awareness, and intuition about what it takes to serve and make the customers' experiences memorable.

The personal experience of one of the authors confirmed that Ritz Carlton's empowering its employees actually works. Upon returning to her room after 10:00 p.m., hungry and tired, she met a worker in the hall and asked where the cafe was located. The woman responded that the cafe was closed and then asked, "What do you want?" Without having to get permission, the employee took ownership and returned shortly with a sandwich, a dill pickle, and iced tea on a silver tray with a red rose. This kind of empowerment is not dependent on finances or organizational size. This same author observed a similar implementation of unanticipated service in a small hotel in West Tennessee. Covey (2004) wrote, "When you truly establish the conditions for empowerment, control is not lost: it is simply transformed into self-control" (p. 256).

> *The goal of a leader is not to exert force but to empower his or her followers; leaders are more like holy men than musclemen.*
>
> ~JAMES MACGREGOR BURNS, AMERICAN HISTORIAN AND AUTHORITY ON LEADERSHIP STUDIES

Delegation and empowerment are built on a foundation of trust. Dialogue between Bennis and Townsend (1995), as recorded in *Reinventing Leadership,* included the following assertions: "Trust binds leaders and followers together, and cannot be bought or mandated. ...the best way to create a trusting environment is to demonstrate trust in those you lead" (p. 61). They added, "A leader can empower people by expecting more of them than they think they can possibly achieve" (p. 74). Parrott (2007) focused on knowing the individuals in the organization so that the leader can assign responsibilities that are consistent with their knowledge base and personal passion. "Your team is made up of knowledge workers. You need to know what is in their heads, and you must care about what is in their hearts. Be attuned to emotion and motivation of the team. You must weigh the needs of the organization and individual team members' concerns" (pp. 16-17).

As a wise leader, delegate responsibilities and empower employees according to their strengths and passion. In this way, people are motivated to want *to do* and *to do* it well.

....

If you want...one year of prosperity, grow grain; ten years of prosperity, grow trees; one hundred years of prosperity, grow people. ~CHINESE PROVERB

....

Aligning Operations

WHAT WILL YOU DO TO PROMOTE EFFECTIVENESS AND EXCELLENCE?

Just as the ship's builders must ensure alignment of all parts of the ship for smooth travel, the captain must also align all operations on board to ensure effective accomplishment of the ship's purpose.

All parts of a ship — the structure, the processes, and the people — must be in alignment for efficient operation. The first part of a ship to be built, the structural keel, serves as the ship's core. It runs along the middle of the ship's bottom, like a spine, serving as a strong, heavily reinforced foundation to support the structure of the ship so as to accomplish its purpose. On some ships, the keel is hydrodynamically designed to increase the ship's performance, helping it move more quickly, smoothly, and efficiently through the water. The body of the ship, known as the hull or shell, is attached to the keel which controls it.

The wheel is the internal instrument used to adjust the ship's rudder to cause the vessel to regulate its course. It is often built with ten spokes that come together in the hub, the center of the wheel, which is ultimately attached to the rudder. Externally, there are instruments, including the beacons of the lighthouse, that are used to inform the ship for course correction.

> *All organizations*
> *are perfectly aligned*
> *to the results they get.*
> ~ ARTHUR W. JONES

Just as the structure of the ship is aligned, so must be the processes on board. Each department, while serving a different function, must operate in concert to provide seamless coordination. Ultimately the alignment of people determines the success or failure of the ship's purpose. From the captain, to the officers, to the crew — all people must understand the goals, have respect for and believe in each other, have expectations and hold one another accountable, and be prepared to work as a team, even doing another's work, especially when a crisis occurs. To avoid danger, the entire crew works together and remains alert to the guidance provided by the lighthouse and other navigational markers.

As with a ship, an effective organization aligns structure, processes, and people. The purpose serves as the core of the organization, giving foundation and direction to the beliefs and values to be understood and shared. Goals, systems, and operations must be grounded in a shared vision of what the desired future will be. Aligning systems is necessary so that the organization is able to move quickly, smoothly, efficiently, and with consistent focus on the purpose, mission, and execution of the organization's vision.

TOOLS FOR ALIGNING OPERATIONS

SKILLSET	Aligning Operations		
TOOL	Vitamin C: Celebrate, Concern, Concentrate		
IMPACT	Individual	✓ Team	✓ Group
PURPOSE	To evaluate the organization's success in remaining centered in the midst of change		

DESCRIPTION

Note: Appropriate for use mid—year, end of year, or at other strategic points

- Identify and list on a chart the areas that are to be reviewed. (May include deemphasizing hierarchy/bureaucracy, sharing leadership, communicating information, organizational data and its use, etc.)

- Evaluate each area using Vitamin Cs: Celebrate, Concern, Concentrate. Definitions:
    - Celebrate—Have made good progress. Identify how to recognize progress.
    - Concern—Improvement is needed. Identify ways to improve.
    - Concentrate—Important to give specific attention. Identify specific means.

....

A leader has the vision and conviction that a dream can be achieved. He inspires the power and energy to get it done. ~ RALPH NADER, AMERICAN POLITICAL ACTIVIST, AUTHOR AND ATTORNEY

....

- Examples:

Area to be Considered	Vitamin Assigned	Follow—Up
Shared Leadership	Celebrate	Have a social event to recognize each person's contribution
Communication	Concern, Concentrate	Identify specific communication needed, to whom, when, and who will do
Data Collection	Celebrate, Concentrate	Thanks to those involved in collection; emphasize importance to continue; add other areas for collection
Use of Data	Concentrate	Study meaning of the data; use data to make changes in priorities or operations
Stakeholders Involvement	Celebrate	At a "thank you" reception share report of stake—holders involvement

DEBRIEF
? Embedded in activity

MATERIALS
✓ Copies of form

Area to be Considered	Vitamin Assigned	Follow—Up

SKILLSET	Aligning Operations		
TOOL	Zoom In – Zoom Out		
IMPACT	Individual	✓ Team	✓ Group
PURPOSE	To emphasize the importance of everyone in the organization seeing the big picture while being responsible for a specific portion		

DESCRIPTION

- Distribute a set of sequential pictures—cards (face down and in random order) to each team. Each participant takes a picture but cannot show it to other team members.

- Have each participant write the part of the story their picture represents, recreating the story without seeing any of the other pictures. (See Materials)

- Have participants read their part of the story to the team.

- Instruct the team to decide on the sequence and read the story in total – without changing any of the script written by team members.

- Choose one or more of the stories to be read aloud.

DEBRIEF

? What did you do when your storyline did not fit team members' stories?

? What attributes were needed in order to recreate the sequence of the team's story's sequence (patience, communication, trust, understanding another's point of view, etc.)?

MATERIALS

✓ Print a set of sequential pictures (cartoon frames are without captions especially effective; steps in a process, etc.)

✓ Place each picture on a separate paper

SKILLSET	Aligning Operations		
TOOL	Big Shoes		
IMPACT	Individual	✓ Team	Group
PURPOSE	To illustrate the need for individuals to work together effectively		

DESCRIPTION

- Choose 2 participants. Care needs to be given in selecting the participants (ability to carry out task safely, age, dexterity, etc.)

- Place the "big shoes" at one end of a large area and ask the participants to put their feet in the shoes.

- Instruct the participants that they have the challenge of moving as a unit across the large area to reach the other end successfully together.

- Give a signal for the participants to begin while others observe their progress.

DEBRIEF

? What did the participants have to do during the activity in order to be successful?

? What role did each team member take in this activity?

? What applications from this activity can be made to the work of teams?

MATERIALS

✓ Two 2" × 2" × 36" boards (such as a heavy yardstick)

✓ 2 pairs of large shoes (either cheap new shoes or disinfected used shoes)

✓ Firmly attach the soles of the shoes (with strong glue) to the boards in such a manner that they face the same way and one shoe from each pair is on each board evenly spaced as its mate.

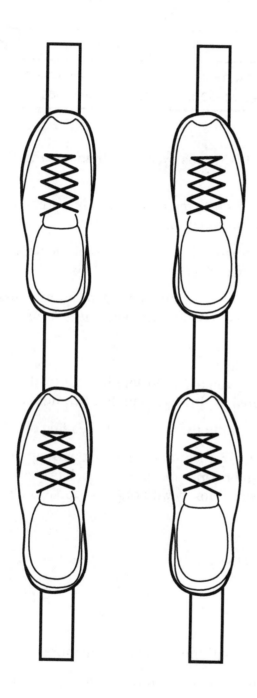

SKILLSET	Aligning Operations		
TOOL	Mission Alignment		
IMPACT	✓ Individual	✓ Team	✓ Group
PURPOSE	To examine if job tasks are in alignment with organizational mission and priorities		

DESCRIPTION

- Note: this activity extends over more than one meeting. See details below.

- Divide participants into teams. (Participants are to bring project cards to a meeting at the end of the month.)

- Guide the participants through a review of the organization's mission, values, and priority goals.

- After the discussion regarding the organization's mission/values/goals, each participant is to review his/her project cards and divide them into three stacks:
  - ↝ Fully Aligns
  - ↝ Partially Aligns, Important but not Critical
  - ↝ Minimal or No Alignment but Required or Mandated

- Place each card under the appropriate heading on the chart.

- Close the activity by recommending that participants assess how much time, money, and people are spent on each project and identify ways to align work more closely with organizational goals.

DEBRIEF

? Embedded in activity

MATERIALS

✓ 4 × 6 note cards

✓ Prior to the meeting (approximately one month):

  - ↝ Prepare printed material regarding the mission, values, and priority goals.

✔ Instruct group participants to keep, for a month, thorough records of all major projects that they are working on.

✔ Provide 4 × 6 cards and explain that they are to use one card for each project.

The information to be noted on the card includes:

- ❧ Project name
- ❧ Dates and number of hours (or partial hours) when work on the project is done
- ❧ Problems encountered, if any, briefly noted
- ❧ Satisfaction level of participant when working on the project

Fully Aligns	Partially Aligns (Important but not Critical)	Minimal or No Alignment (Required or Mandated)

....

Genuine success does not come from proclaiming our values, but from consistently putting them into daily action. ~ MICHAEL O'CONNOR

....

SKILLSET	Aligning Operations		
TOOL	Roping		
IMPACT	Individual	✓ Team	✓ Group
PURPOSE	To provide a physical example of the importance of alignment.		

DESCRIPTION

- Divide a large group into smaller teams of 8–12 participants.

- Identify an observer and a facilitator for each team.

- Have each team select a leader and have everyone in the team blind—fold themselves, including the leader.

- Place the 40 feet of rope in front of each group, in a straight line or double line, depending on the number in the group.

- The facilitator will explain:

  - ❧ This activity must be completed without talking;
  - ❧ there is a rope somewhere in front of them;
  - ❧ without removing blindfolds, the team needs to walk forward until their feet find the rope;
  - ❧ when a team member's feet find the rope, they are to call out "Found it." *This is the only time anyone in the group except the leader can talk.*
  - ❧ Everyone picks up the rope. While everyone is holding to the rope, the leader must help the group align the ends and then make a square.

- Have the facilitator watch to assure no one gets hurt or wanders off too far.

- Have the observer record interactions and how teams align themselves to complete the task.

- Allow 30 minutes for the task.

- At the end of 30 minutes, the observer will announce "Stop." The group removes blindfolds. The group that has the best square or rectangle is recognized.

DEBRIEF

? What caused this activity to be difficult?

? How did the team work together?

? What was/was not helpful about the instructions?

? What made alignment difficult?

? How did this exercise illustrate the difficulty of organizational alignment, etc.?

MATERIALS

✓ 40 feet of rope for each team (8–12 participants)

✓ Blindfolds for each participant

✓ Open area outside, such as a park, baseball or football field, etc.

....

My own definition of leadership is this: The capacity and the will to rally men and women to a common purpose and the character which inspires confidence.

~ GENERAL MONTGOMERY, BRITISH ARMY OFFICER

....

SKILLSET	Aligning Operations		
TOOL	Puzzled		
IMPACT	Individual	✓ Team	✓ Group
PURPOSE	To assist understanding that parts affect the whole and that individual members of teams make contributions to the whole		

DESCRIPTION

- Divide into teams of 4–6.

- Provide a bag of puzzle pieces to each team. Do not disclose that the pieces of the puzzle in each bag have been altered. (See Materials.)

- Tell participants that the objective is to put the puzzles together in less than 5 minutes.

- Tell them to begin and set timer for 5 minutes.

- Tips:

  - ∞ Decline to help, if asked.
  - ∞ Encourage them to use any resources available.
  - ∞ If they ask permission to work with other groups, be noncommittal. Say, "You know what your objective is, do what you need to do to achieve it."

DEBRIEF

? How did the parts have the potential to affect the whole?

? What impact did the wrong pieces have on achieving the objective?

? Would a picture of the completed puzzle have helped?

? How does this relate to values, mission, and goals?

MATERIALS

✓ Timer

✓ One children's puzzle of approximately 25 pieces for each team/ small group

✓ A bag for each puzzle's pieces

✓ Assemble bags in advance

  ❧ Place all the puzzle pieces for each puzzle in a separate bag.
  ❧ Remove four pieces from each bag.
  ❧ Place two pieces in other bags, each piece in a different bag.
  ❧ Discard two pieces so they are not included in play.

....

No one can be the best at everything. But when all of us combine our talents, we can be the best at virtually anything. ~ DON WARD, BRITISH COMEDY ENTREPRENEUR

....

SKILLSET	Aligning Operations		
TOOL	CPR—S		
IMPACT	✓ Individual	✓ Team	Group
PURPOSE	To identify current health of the organization		

DESCRIPTION

- Ask participants to consider specific areas of the organization including:

  - ∾ Communication
  - ∾ Processes/Procedures
  - ∾ Reward System
  - ∾ Structure

- Post charts — one for each area to be considered (provided).

- Considering each area individually, participants identify what has been done well and list them under PLUS on the chart. (Caution participants that names or positions of individuals cannot be used.) Have a scribe record ideas on the specific chart.

- Considering the same area, participants identify what could be improved and list them under DELTA* on the chart. (Caution participants that names or positions of individuals cannot be used.) Have a scribe record ideas on the specific chart.

- Move to the next area and complete the same steps on another chart.

- Continue considering areas until all are completed.

DEBRIEF

? What are the areas for celebration?

? What improvements are needed? What should the action plan be to address it?

MATERIALS

✓ Chart Paper

✓ Markers

✓ One form per area of consideration

*In *astrodynamics* a △ or **delta** is a measure of the amount of "effort" that is needed to change from one *trajectory* to another by making an *orbital maneuver*. Retrieved from http://en.wikipedia.org/wiki/Delta—v

Area for Consideration:	
+ PLUS (What is working)	**△ DELTA** (What could be improved)

....

The way management treats the associates is exactly how the associates will then treat the customer. ~ SAM WALTON, FOUNDER OF WALMART

....

SKILLSET	Aligning Operations		
TOOL	Keep the Pattern, Keep the Ideas		
IMPACT	Individual	Team	✓ Group
PURPOSE	To demonstrate organizational alignment of concepts and practices		

DESCRIPTION

- Have all participants stand in a circle with their hands open and palms up. After the participant tosses the Koosh Ball to someone else, s/he will close their hands and hold their hands in front of them. This will indicate they have already had the ball.

- Create the pattern by tossing the Koosh Ball to someone in the circle. Each participant in turn tosses it to another person in the circle. Once this pattern is set, it cannot be changed during the activity.

- Toss the Koosh Ball around the circle until everyone has had the ball once; the last person to have the Koosh Ball will toss the ball to the leader, and the activity is completed.

- Check to make sure that everyone knows to whom they tossed the ball. Replicate the pattern a second time. If someone cannot remember, stop to figure out the pattern again.

- For practice, start by having the participants name different states. Have someone begin by tossing the ball to the leader while saying, "Washington." The leader says, "Tennessee" and tosses the ball to another participant. Continue tossing the ball until everyone has had a turn.

- Ask the participants to brainstorm ideas on a given topic as the ball is tossed. Identify a specific issue that needs to be addressed within the organization (e.g., Ideas for Involving Stakeholders, Improving Communications, Marketing Strategies, etc.). If someone cannot think of something to say, they can repeat what someone else has said, but the challenge is to say something new.

- List the ideas that were generated during the activity.

DEBRIEF

? Embedded in activity

MATERIALS
- ✓ Koosh Ball
- ✓ Chart paper
- ✓ Markers

....

The true mark of a leader is the willingness to stick with a bold course of action — an unconventional business strategy, a unique product development roadmap, a controversial marketing campaign — even as the rest of the world wonders why you're not marching in step with the status quo. In other words, real leaders are happy to zig while others zag. They understand that in an era of hyper-competition and non-stop disruption, the only way to stand out from the crowd is to stand for something special. ~ BILL TAYLOR, CO-FOUNDER AND EDITOR OF *FAST COMPANY MAGAZINE, FORMER EDITOR OF HARVARD BUSINESS REVIEW*

....

SKILLSET	Aligning Operations		
TOOL	Looking From the Outside In		
IMPACT	Individual	✓ Team	✓ Group
PURPOSE	To evaluate goal accomplishment		

DESCRIPTION

Notes:

This activity requires extended time (2–4 hours) to fully capture the current status of the organization.

In order for this fishbowl activity to be successful, everyone must have a high level of trust and be assured that there will be no negative repercussions from candid dialogue.

It is important that both agreements are expressed and discrepancies are uncovered. This activity may be used with other important questions about which clarity of organizational direction is needed.

- Have the members of the leadership team sit in chairs in a circle.

- Have the second tier of organizational leadership sit in chairs directly behind for the purpose of hearing the discussion by the leadership team.

- Instruct each member of the leadership team to discuss the two most pressing organizational goals for the year, their action plans to address the goals, and progress made toward reaching the goals.

- Instruct the participants in the second tier not to comment, but only listen and take notes.

- At the end of an hour, the second tier participants change seats with the leadership team. Again, this time the leadership team members are in the second tier and are not allowed to comment, but only listen and take notes.

- The second tier participants discuss what they heard the leadership team say, whether or not there is understanding of organizational goals at the next organizational level, and if there is agreement that progress is being made or if there are misunderstandings or discrepancies.

- Have the participants lead a discussion to record summary results of the fishbowl conversation on an enlarged chart similar to the one provided.

DEBRIEF
? Embedded in activity

MATERIALS
✓ Chart

✓ Markers

✓ Set up circle of chairs

✓ Notify participants of expectations

Understanding	Discrepancy
Progress	**Lack of Progress**

SKILLSET	Aligning Operations		
TOOL	Four Corners		
IMPACT	Individual	✓ Team	✓ Group
PURPOSE	To consider personal alignment with the organization's mission		

DESCRIPTION

- Ask participants to silently review the copy of the organizational information (include mission, values, vision, services, and structure).

- Give consideration to the four words that are on the chart papers in the four corners of the room (MEANING, ACTION, RELATIONSHIPS, STRUCTURE).

- Instruct participants to select the one word that they feel is most indicative of their own personal mission.

- Have participants select one "four corner" word and move to the corner where that chart is displayed. For 3–5 minutes, the group in each corner will discuss the reasons they chose that "four corner" word as it relates to organizational mission.

- Have each group select a reporter to offer the "gist" of why the participants in the group chose the word.

DEBRIEF

? How does personal mission impact organizational mission?

? What happens when personal and organizational missions are aligned? Not aligned?

MATERIALS NEEDED

✓ Copies of organizational information that includes mission, values, vision, services, and structure for each participant.

✓ Four sheets of chart paper with one of the following words as a heading and a definition of each. Use one sheet for each word:

- ✑ MEANING—Personal satisfaction
- ✑ ACTION—Ability to be involved
- ✑ RELATIONSHIPS—Opportunity to work with others

❧ STRUCTURE—Understanding of roles and responsibilities

....

The quality of a leader is reflected in the standards they set for themselves. ~ RAY KROC, FOUNDER OF MCDONALDS

....

SKILLSET	Aligning Operations		
TOOL	Fix the Problem		
IMPACT	✓ Individual	✓ Team	Group
PURPOSE	To practice evaluating a situation and creating solutions to problems that will cause the organization to be more effective		

DESCRIPTION

- Explain that each team will read and analyze one of three scenarios (provided) and make recommendations about how to deal with the problems that are presented in order to cause the organization to be more effective.

- Indicate the time limits for the activity — approximately 30 minutes.

- Distribute copies of one scenario to each team. (You may prefer to create scenarios that relate specifically to your organization.)

- Provide time for participants to read, analyze, and create solutions to the problems described in the scenario given to their team.

- Ask each team/group to identify a reporter and to write their solutions on the graphic organizer.

- Encourage each team to identify a minimum of eight possible actions.

- When work time is completed, ask each reporter, in turn, to briefly explain problems and solutions that the team recommended.

DEBRIEF

? What were the challenges to develop many possible solutions?

? What were the easy solutions, and what were the better solutions?

? Was there alignment or similarities between the two solutions?

MATERIALS

✓ One scenario for each participant organized by team

✓ One copy of the graphic organizer (provided) for each team

SCENARIOS FOR "FIX THE PROBLEM"

1. NYY Engineering is an engineering company in Boston. They build military equipment on a five year contract that they received three years ago. The engineers are informed by the accounting department what they are able to spend on materials and labor hours. All estimates of the bid given to receive the contract were compiled by the accounting department. NYY is currently behind schedule and has been hearing rumors that their contract may be terminated before it expires. How would you fix the problem with NYY Engineering?

2. The superintendent of XYZ school district has noticed that teachers in the district use their unused sick days at the end of every school year and that students' test scores begin to drop about the same time. Teachers in XYZ school district receive five sick days for the year and any unused days are forfeited at the end of the school year. What would you recommend to the superintendent to do to address this problem and what should be the process for implementation and communication?

3. The IT Computer Company has two offices, one in Chicago and one in Los Angeles. The VP for Marketing oversees the Chicago office and all of the departments in Chicago including marketing, human resources, and the customer support center. The VP for Product Development oversees the LA office and all of the departments there, including research and development, sales, and accounting. The President/Founder of the company is not active in running the company and has left most decisions to the discretion of the VPs. The VPs have been discussing several issues: products are designed and being sold before any marketing for the product has been done; customer complaints/problems reach the research and development team only twice a month for them to develop fixes to flaws discovered in programs, and human resources is only in LA once a month to conduct interviews for vacant positions. The VPs have contacted the President with the issues they are facing and have been given permission to take any action, other than selling the company or closing it down, to solve their issues. What would you do?

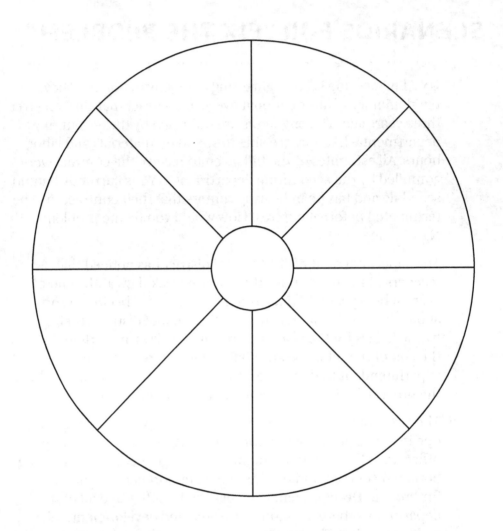

He who would learn to fly one day must first learn to stand and walk and climb and dance. One cannot fly into flying.

~ FRIEDRICH NIETZSCHE, GERMAN PHILOLOGIST AND COMPOSER

SKILLSET	Aligning Operations		
TOOL	Halls, Walls, & Climate		
IMPACT	✓ Individual	✓ Team	✓ Group
PURPOSE	To evaluate if the physical spaces and the climate of the organization express the organization's values		

DESCRIPTION

- Take a walk through the organization's physical space.

- Have participants envision themselves as strangers walking through the organization's building.

- Have participants list everything on the organization's walls and in the halls and note impressions about the environment.

- After the walk, have a scribe compile the notes on a large chart.

- Review how the organization's mission/goals/values/desired image are reflected.

- Encourage participants to identify things that are not aligned with the organization's mission/goals/values/desired image and brainstorm how to more accurately portray the organization in the displays, considering all stakeholders.

DEBRIEF

? Embedded in activity

MATERIALS

✓ Chart paper

✓ Markers

BASED ON ARTICLE BY

Hoerr, T.R. (2006). The schoolhouse at midnight. *Educational leadership,* 673, 86–88.

SKILLSET	Aligning Operations		
TOOL	Taking Stock		
IMPACT	✓ Individual	✓ Team	✓ Group
PURPOSE	To "take stock" before starting new projects, when completing tasks, or when momentum slows		

DESCRIPTION

- Explain that SWOT stands for Strengths, Weaknesses, Opportunities, and Threats. Indicate that the purpose is to identify possibilities and potential roadblocks that can be dealt with as needed. The SWOT can also put problems or issues into perspective. See diagram provided.

- Explain that Force Field Analysis is a tool that helps decision-making by examining the "forces" that are working for and against an issue, project, suggested change, etc. See diagram.

- Divide the participants into two teams of 4–8 members. If there are more participants, 4 or 6 teams can be formed.

- **Team 1** — Begin by using the SWOT analysis having participants list strengths related to an identified issue, a goal, or a problem. Ask: What do we do well? What strengths do our people have?

  - Second, have team members list weaknesses. Ask: Where do we need to improve? What skills are needed?
  - Third, list possible opportunities, such as a grant, new technology, training, or other resources, events, and people to help. Ask: What are interesting trends that we know about? What advantages and resources do we have in place?
  - Finally, list any threats to success. Ask: What obstacles do we face? What should we avoid? What roadblocks might get in our way?

- **Team 2** — Using the Force Field Analysis diagram, have the team members identify all the possible forces (issues, personnel, skills, market influences, supply and demand, etc.) working for and in favor of the issue, goal or problem. Encourage the participants to brainstorm beyond the obvious.

  Second, have the team members identify possible forces that are working against the issue, goal, or problem. Encourage the team to make sure each force working for the issue has a force which opposes it. There may be some which do not have corresponding forces.

Ask: How does each constructive force relate to the negative force? Why does one outweigh the other?

Are there forces working for the issue that do not have corresponding negative forces? What are the causes behind that happening?

What would be the possible suggested outcomes of the issue, goal, or problem?

How does this impact our work?

DEBRIEF

? What types of information are gathered from the two tools?

? How can this information influence our decision making?

? How can we avoid limits or remove such threats so that progress and work can continue?

MATERIALS

✓ Prepare chart(s) for each team

ADAPTED FROM

Gregory, G., & Kuzmich, L. (2007). *Teacher teams that get results: 61 strategies for sustaining and renewing professional learning communities.* Thousand Oaks, CA: Corwin Press.

SWOT
....

Topic, Issue, Project:	
Strengths	**Weaknesses**
Opportunities	**Threats**

FORCE FIELD ANALYSIS

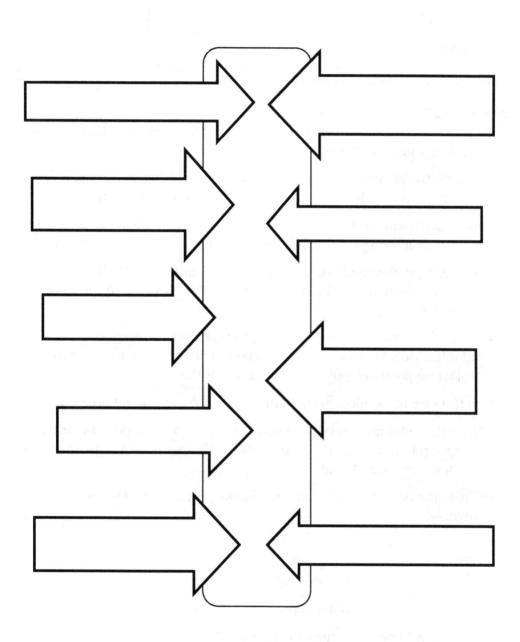

SKILLSET	Aligning Operations		
TOOL	Which Direction?		
IMPACT	Individual	✓ Team	✓ Group
PURPOSE	To assist participants in evaluating if the tasks in a department or organization are in alignment		

DESCRIPTION

- Facilitate a discussion with the group as a reminder of organizational mission, values, and goals.

- Explain the Fishbone Diagram* (provided) as it is used to visually show alignment or misalignment of tasks within an organization.

- Ask participants to review their project lists and make notes indicating how well each project/task addresses the mission, values, or goals.

- Ask each person to identify a project that is aligned with the mission and write the name of the project on an arrow directed to the front of the fish.

- Ask each person to identify a project that is NOT well-aligned with the organization's mission, values, and goals and write the name of the project on an arrow pointed to the back of the fish.

- As time permits, allow participants to include additional projects.

- Once the fishbone has been completed, use it as a visual depiction for the group to assess what is and is not in alignment with organizational mission, values, and goals.

Note: This may be used to eliminate or change projects that are not in alignment.

DEBRIEF

? What are the generalizations that can be made?

? How does this inform the department for future work?

? What should be done, undone, initiated, etc.?

MATERIALS/PRIOR PREPARATION:

✓ Charts for each participant or each group

✓ Prior to the activity, create a fishbone diagram large enough for the group to see and to write on when the diagram is posted. Several diagrams may be needed for very large groups.

෴ Step 1

෴ Step 2

෴ Step 3, etc.

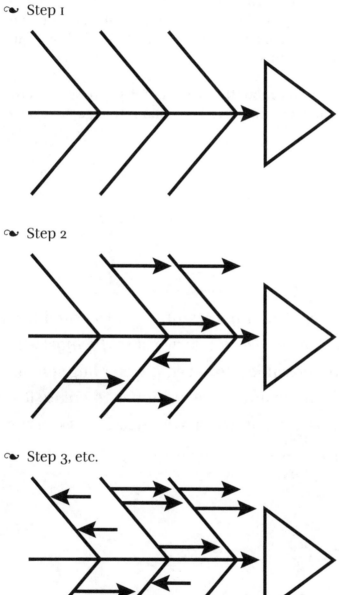

Note: Arrows directed to the front of the head of the fish indicate alignment with goals and those directed to the back represent misalignment.

*The Fishbone Diagram was created by Kaoru Ishikawa (b.1915—d.1989), a Japanese University professor, who worked with Nissan. The diagram is used to provide a visual of alignment and cause and effect. The Fishbone Diagram has been used extensively in Total Quality Management programs.

Additional information about the Fishbone Diagram can be retrieved from https://www.google.com/search?q=fishbone+diagram

. . . .

Alignment is critical if you want to get the right things done and move your organization forward in the most effective and efficient way possible. However, it won't happen on its own. As a leader, you must take the initiative to create it. ~ MICHAEL HYATT, AUTHOR AND FORMER CEO OF THOMAS NELSON PUBLISHERS

. . . .

SKILLSET	Aligning Operations		
TOOL	From Values to Actions		
IMPACT	✔ Individual	✔ Team	✔ Group
PURPOSE	To identify the progression from an organizational value to institutional practice		

DESCRIPTION

- Create teams of 4–6 participants. (This may be used as an individual activity also.)

- Distribute a copy of the Values to Actions worksheet to each participant.

- Identify a specific organizational value to be considered for this activity and ask participants to place it in the box corresponding to the word "Values" on the worksheet. (e.g., On the sample provided, the value is identified as "Exploration.") You may wish to assign a different value to each team.

- Ask each individual or group to complete the worksheet by writing a statement of belief, vision, mission, goal, and action in the boxes corresponding to each steps.

- Have each team explain their completed form to the entire group.

DEBRIEF

? Are there any values that were suggested that are not appropriate to our organization?

? What challenges did you experience in completing the worksheet?

? Was completing any of the steps easier or more difficult than others?

? How can others see the organizational values in action?

MATERIALS

✔ Copies of the Values to Actions worksheet for each participant.

✔ List of values of specific organization

Sample chart and Work chart from: Center for Leadership in School Reform 2/13/95 I-G

VALUES TO ACTIONS SAMPLE

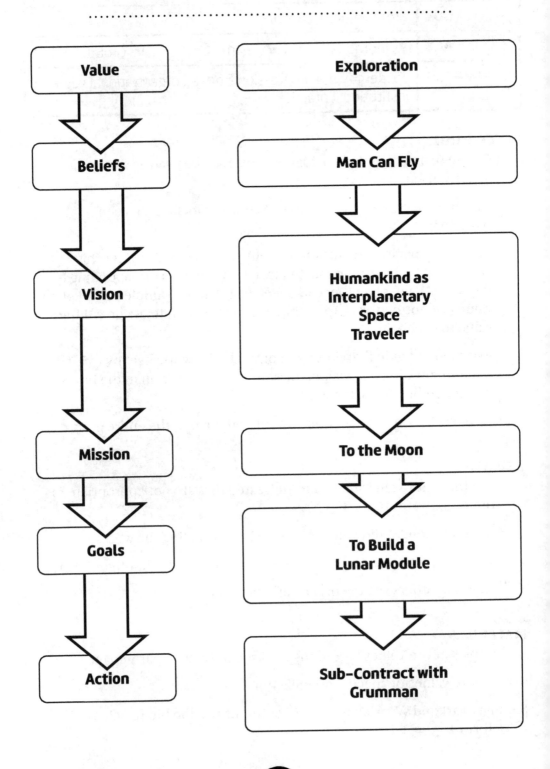

Value	Exploration
Beliefs	Man Can Fly
Vision	Humankind as Interplanetary Space Traveler
Mission	To the Moon
Goals	To Build a Lunar Module
Action	Sub-Contract with Grumman

VALUES TO ACTIONS

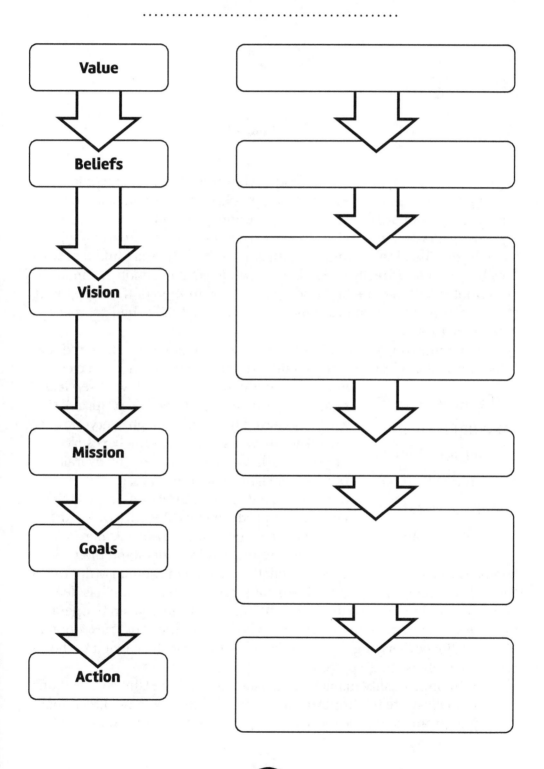

Value

Beliefs

Vision

Mission

Goals

Action

AO–37
191

ANCHORS

. . . .

As an effective organizational leader, your priorities must include aligning operations. Policies, structures, workers' beliefs and tasks, etc. need to align with organizational purpose and direction.

"No organization has a right to exist," according to Jim Stuart (1999) when he discussed that companies must prove who they are and that what they have to offer is really needed. In *Reframing Organizations*, Bolman and Deal (2008) identified the first undergirding assumption of their proposed *structural frame* as "Organizations exist to achieve established goals and objectives" (p. 45).

Jim Clemmer (1993), the CEO of Achieve International, emphasized the importance of structure when he said, "Your organization needs a clear and consistent understanding of what service/qualities mean and how to deliver it" (p. 26). He further asserted that even though everyone in the organization wants to provide the best service or product, they often do not see the overall purpose or vision, and, therefore, everyone does not go in the same direction. In a training PowerPoint produced by ORACLE (2011b), Kaplan and Norton are quoted as saying, "A mere 7% of employees today fully understand their company's business strategies and what's expected of them in order to help achieve company goals." From all appearances, this perception has declined and will continue to do so unless intentional attention is given to operational alignment. Stephen M. R. Covey (2006) in *The Speed of Trust*, quoted Arthur W. Jones as saying, "All organizations are perfectly aligned to the results they are getting" (p. 238).

> *If everyone is moving forward together, then the success takes care of itself.*
>
> ~ ANONYMOUS

In promoting quality management, Deming used the Ishikawa fishbone diagram to illustrate the importance of the need for the same directional flow by all people and processes in an organization. Of his 14 points of Total

Quality Management, Deming's number one point was *creating constancy of purpose*. Baldrige.com reported that Deming believed that 80-95% of an organization's problems are systems problems, not people problems. Similarly, Clemmer (1993) noted that 85% of the time errors result from the systems, processes, structure, or practices of the organization; only 15% of problems can be traced to people not doing what they are supposed to do.

In aligning processes, it is important that you break down barriers, that is, remove the silo effect, between teams and departments to constantly align the systems for producing goods or services. Protecting turf tends to be a natural behavior of departments within organizations. Removing that mindset requires you to give focused attention to developing collaboration, shared vision, and shared resources so that, as Ashkenas, Ulrich, Jick, and Kerr (2002) in *The Boundaryless Organization* stated, the organization can "show one face to the customer" (p. 128). Clemmer (1993) described ineffective process when he stated that the work of too many people is not part of the managed process, never being

> *On the great ship, everyone ought to be prepared to take the helm.*
>
> ~ MARGARET LEWIS, PRESIDENT HCA CAPITAL DIVISION

> effectively planned/organized as part of a cross-functional picture. The same lack of clear focus often fuses departments in haphazard ways. Materials, information, paperwork, and customers are often tossed from one vertical chimney to another — passing the buck. (p. 243)

As with alignment of structure and operations, alignment of people is essential for success of organizational purpose. Albrecht (1994) suggested that executives cannot achieve organizational success alone. They must develop a "constellation of teams to bring talents and resources to bear on the challenge of creating superior customer value and sustaining a competitive advantage" (p. 93). Senge (2006) identified five core disciplines needed by individuals to assist organizations in aligning their systems to achieve desired results. The five disciplines are:

1. personal learning by individuals,

2. removing the internal images that limit teams in thinking and acting,

3. developing a view of the organization's future that is embraced by everyone,

4. building processes that result in team learning, and

5. systems thinking that results in organizational alignment when all the other disciplines are practiced throughout the organization.

In order to develop the business you desire, Parrott (2007) identified four essentials that must be in alignment:

"Production— Implement a winning strategy;

People—Build a professional team;

Processes—Improve the way work is done;

Potential—Expand the capacity of the organization" (p. 54).

In a podcast entitled *How Leaders Can Create Alignment*, Hyatt (2012) suggested that leaders create alignment in teams by three practices: Contact, Communication, and Connection. The importance of frequent contact is emphasized, including meetings, personal contact, and just walking around. Communication includes verbalizing the mission and vision and having dialogue. Connection must be evident so that people will know and trust the leader's heart and be committed to helping the leader succeed. All this was summarized in the statement: "You can buy their presence, but you can't buy their heart" (Podcast No. 015). Hyatt continued:

> Alignment is that optimal state in which strategy, employees, customers, and key processes work in concert to propel growth and profits. Aligned organizations enjoy greater customer and employee satisfaction and produce superior returns to share-holders. Aligned companies focus employees and their work on key goals. They de-emphasize hierarchy and distribute leadership by apportioning authority, information, and customer data. In an aligned organization, every employee — from the executive suite to the loading dock — understands not only the strategy and goals of the business, but also how his or her work contributes to them. Everyone can articulate what the needs of the customer are and what his or her unit must do to satisfy them. According to Fred Smith, the chairman of FedEX, "Alignment is the essence of management". (Podcast No. 015)

Through strategic planning, the mission, vision, values, beliefs, and goals inform the organization's action plan, aligning the operations to accomplish the delivery of goods or services to satisfy the needs of targeted consumers. Aligning processes eliminates silos and the "lone wolf" so that each process, regardless of independent function, creates interdependency in providing effectively for the overall product. Aligning people with the organization's purpose requires not only that they know the expectations of their job functions, but also that they have the training and skills required to accomplish assigned tasks and understand how their roles fit into the overall success of the organization. A culture must exist that respects the job function regardless of perceived importance and emphasizes the necessity for team work, realizing that all jobs are honorable and necessary. This will reinforce the importance of each role in accomplishing the organization's defining purpose. Your role as leader is to communicate these essential skillsets of an effective organization to your co-workers.

Starting the Journey

HOW WILL YOU BEGIN?

The ship's log provides a draft and eventually an official record
of the ship's plan to accomplish the purpose of the voyage.

In preparation for voyages, the captain and crew of commercial ships, naval vessels, and seaworthy personal crafts must conduct advance planning. This includes reviewing static maps as a reference guide to understand formations, coast lines, and unique characteristics of the land mass along which the ship will travel. They also review navigational charts for the purpose of identifying what is not visible to the naked eye: water depth, hazards such as sand bars, sea currents, and channel markers including lighthouses and buoys, and other existing conditions. Using the information from the charts, the crew creates a "rough" or "scrap" log, which serves as a planning draft of the ship's course, speed, location, and other data. Entries to the rough log are made daily throughout the trip with revisions as conditions change and planning continues. The rough log is converted into the "smooth" log that becomes the official record of the voyage. The smooth log is considered permanent to serve as a historical record, analogous to a black box, so no erasures are permitted.

Productivity is never an accident. It is always the result of a commitment to excellence, intelligent planning, and focused effort.

~ PAUL J. MEYER

In beginning the organizational journey, the leader with the selected leadership team must engage in short and long-term planning. Scanning the environment for outside factors that influence the organization and the direction the leaders should take serves as a useful map. Scanning the organization for factors not immediately visible becomes the chart by which leaders gather information specific to the conditions within the organization such as potential, opportunities, challenges, constraints, resources, and skills of the people involved. With this information, leaders begin to craft the "rough log" that eventually translates into long-term goals for the organization. Short-term planning identifies specific activities that will move the organization closer to achieving the goals. Recording the outcomes provides evidence of progress made toward the goals, and this serves as the official record, "smooth log," for the organization.

· ·

We are what we repeatedly do. Excellence, then, is not an act but a habit. ~ ARISTOTLE, GREEK PHILOSOPHER

· ·

TOOLS FOR STARTING THE JOURNEY

SKILLSET	Starting the Journey		
TOOL	Internal vs. External		
IMPACT	✓ Individual	✓ Team	✓ Group
PURPOSE	To examine both the internal and external forces that impact the operations of organizations		

DESCRIPTION

- Explain that SWOT stands for Strengths, Weaknesses (Internal), Opportunities, and Threats (External). Indicate that the purpose is to identify possibilities and potential roadblocks that can be dealt with as needed. The SWOT can also put problems or issues into perspective. See diagram provided. If working with a large group, may want to divide into teams of 6–10 participants.

- Begin using the SWOT analysis by having participants list strengths related to an identified issue, a goal, or a problem. Ask: What do we do well? What strengths do our people have?

- Second, list weaknesses. Ask: Where do we need to improve? What skills are needed?

- Third, list possible opportunities, such as a grant, new technology, training, or other resources, events, and people to help. Ask: What are interesting trends that we know about? What advantages and resources do we have in place?

- Finally, list any threats to success. Ask: What obstacles do we face? What should we avoid? What roadblocks might get in our way?

- Follow-up with discussion about how to avoid limits or remove such threats so that progress and work can continue.

DEBRIEF

? What does this information indicate about the future of the company?

? What planning can be done considering this information?

? Are there any issues that can be addressed immediately?

MATERIALS

✓ Chart paper

✓ Markers

✓ SWOT charts – one per team if group is divided into teams

....

There are no short cuts to "being the best"; it always involves big dreams and the unwavering commitment to pay the price through discipline and hard work. ~ ANONYMOUS

....

SWOT

. . . .

Topic, Issue, Project:

Strengths:	Weaknesses:
Opportunities:	Threats:

ADAPTED FROM

Gregory, G., & Kuzmich, L. (2007). *Teacher teams that get results: 61 strategies for sustaining and renewing professional learning communities.* Thousand Oaks, CA: Corwin Press.

SKILLSET	Starting the Journey		
TOOL	Deliberate Deliberation		
IMPACT	✓ Individual	✓ Team	✓ Group
PURPOSE	To identify the areas to be addressed in an organization		

DESCRIPTION

- Distribute the "Deliberate Deliberation" form to each employee (provided).

- Have each person complete the form and return it to a neutral place or person. In order to secure responses from everyone, have a roster for the employees to initial when submitting the form.

- Collate all responses.

- Review information with the leadership team.

- Share trends, as appropriate, with employees.

DEBRIEF

? Are there any noticeable trends?

? How can the organization use this information?

? Is there something in the organization that needs to be changed?

? How can this information inform the goals of the organization?

? If appropriate, develop a timeline per the top 3–4 items.

MATERIALS

✓ Individual inventory per participant

✓ Envelope or box for completed forms

✓ Roster of all employees to initial when submitting the form

....

Luck happens when preparation meets opportunity.

~ ANSEL ADAMS, AMERICAN PHOTOGRAPHER AND ENVIRONMENTALIST

....

DELIBERATE DELIBERATION

An important part of becoming the organization that we desire is being able to consider candidly where it is at this time. Please respond frankly to the items below, giving thought to your responses. This is to be done anonymously. Please return it to the designated location. Remember, this information will be used to make decisions about the direction of the organization. Please list responses by priority.

List the five qualities/activities/programs that are strengths of this organization.

1.

2.

3.

4.

5.

List the five qualities/activities/programs that are weaknesses of this organization.

1.

2.

3.

4.

5.

List the five qualities/activities/programs that should be implemented.

1.

2.

3.

4.

5.

List the five qualities/activities/programs that should be removed.

      1.

      2.

      3.

      4.

      5.

   Please share any additional comments that you feel are important for the success of this organization. (Use the back of this sheet if necessary.)

....

Progress has little to do with speed, but much to do with direction. ~ ANONYMOUS

....

SKILLSET	Starting the Journey		
TOOL	Digging Deeper		
IMPACT	Individual	✔ Team	✔ Group
PURPOSE	To organize information and stimulate thinking power		

DESCRIPTION

- Group participants into teams of 6–8 members.

- Instruct participants in the process of "mind mapping". (There are many examples online. Two are illustrated on the next pages.) Emphasize that there are numerous ways to illustrate the brainstorming process graphically.

- Explain or gain consensus about the issue to be addressed.

- Assign one issue, concern, or idea to each team.

- Give chart paper to teams. Ask teams to put a word or symbol for the starting point. Have a scribe for each team capture all ideas expressed (no censoring).

  - ❧ Link thoughts by lines, arrows, dotted lines, etc. Color can be used to organize ideas, stimulate new thoughts, or just to add interest.
  - ❧ Ask teams to share their mind map on the topic assigned.

DEBRIEF

? What are the possibilities that this map illustrates?

? Are there any steps expressed?

? What might be the outlier ideas? Are any worth exploring deeper?

? What should be done with the information gathered?

MATERIALS

✔ Chart paper

✔ Markers

✔ Identify one or more issues, concerns, or ideas to be discussed

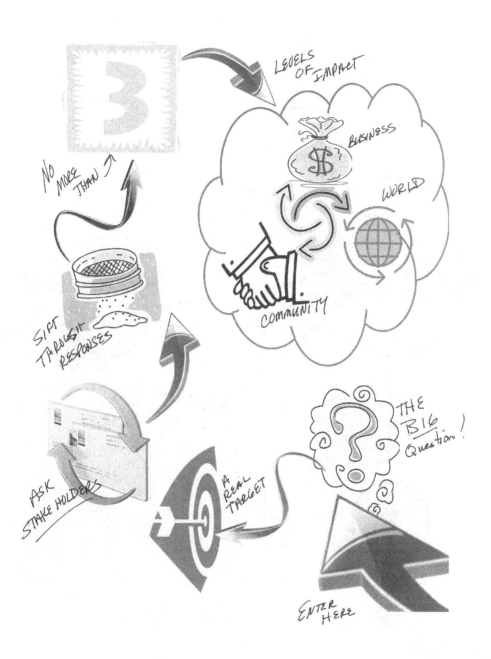

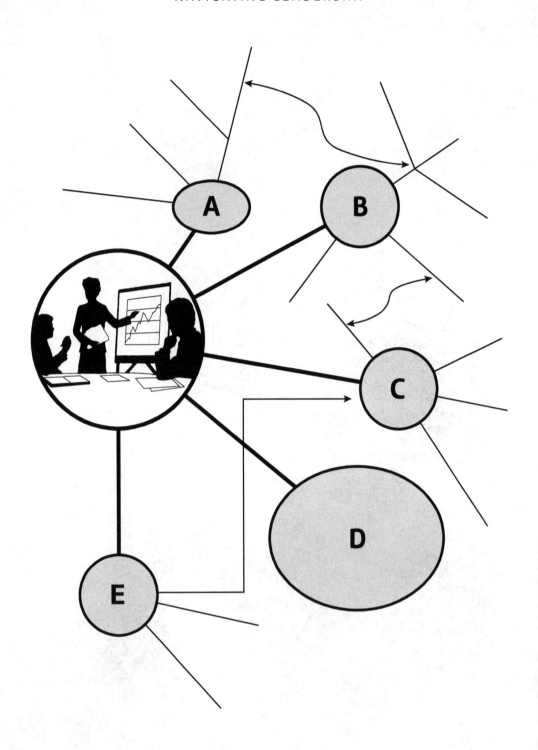

SKILLSET	Starting the Journey		
TOOL	Maps, Charts, Blueprints, and Recipes		
IMPACT	Individual	✔ Team	✔ Group
PURPOSE	To illustrate the need to use the correct tool to get to the right destination		

DESCRIPTION

- Divide the group into four teams. Give each team chart paper and markers.

- Assign one of the tools for their work: maps, charts, blueprints, or recipes.

- Have the teams divide their chart paper into three columns and entitle each column with:

Types   **Purposes**   **Provides**

- Ask the team members to brainstorm the different types of their assigned tool, the different purposes for it, and what information it provides.

- Challenge each team to discuss the advantages and disadvantages of using the assigned tool.

- Ask each team to identify four points of information.

- Have each team report to the total group.

DEBRIEF

? Was there any overlap for the purpose of the four different tools?

? Can one tool be used in place of another? Why or why not?

? What would be the outcomes of having only one or two of the tools?

? How can this information be used in organizational planning?

MATERIALS
✔ Chart paper

✔ Markers

SKILLSET	Starting the Journey		
TOOL	Four Lenses		
IMPACT	✓ Individual	✓ Team	✓ Group
PURPOSE	To investigate how goals are perceived through different attributes		

DESCRIPTION

- Divide the participants into 3 groups.

- Identify the top three goals of the organization. (If more than three goals have been set, choose the top three. Keep the processing groups to 4–5 people. More than one group can process the same goal as another group.)

- Give each group a copy of the chart (provided). Chart paper can be used.

- Explain that participants are to process the goal through the lenses of the four identified attributes.

- Have the participants process the goal from each of the attributes, asking the question, "What _____ (competence, character, compassion, courage) will it require of us to be able to complete this goal with excellence?"

- Have the groups process these questions writing the main ideas in the charts.

- Have each team report to the total group.

DEBRIEF

? What are the common themes that emerged?

? How does this information inform our operations?

? What can we do (or stop doing) Monday morning in order to move ahead in accomplishing the goal?

MATERIALS

✓ Goals of organization

✓ Copies of chart per participant

✔ Chart paper
✔ Markers

Goal

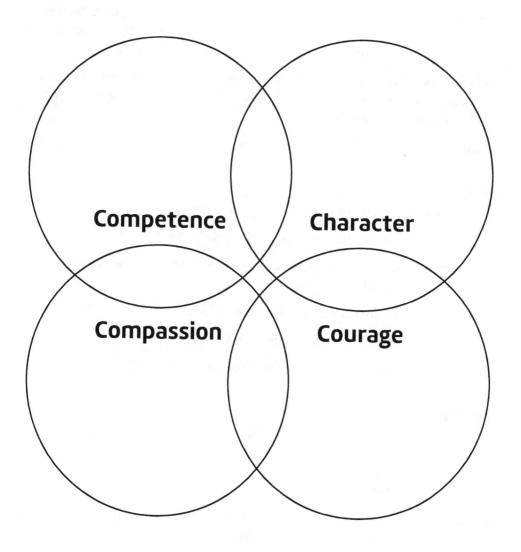

SKILLSET	Starting the Journey		
TOOL	Swap		
IMPACT	Individual	✓ Team	✓ Group
PURPOSE	To generate numerous ideas about topics of concern		

DESCRIPTION

- Give each participant a card on which is written a question. (Sample provided)

- Give instructions to participants to pose the question that is on his/her card to another random participant. Then the partner poses his/her question. After both partners have responded to the questions, they swap cards and find another random partner and repeat.

- Hint: to expedite the process of finding a random partner, when the partners are finished, they raise their hand so others in the group can locate another partner.

- Allow 20–30 minutes for the process.

DEBRIEF

? What were the themes that developed?

? Were there any urgent issues mentioned?

? Are there some issues which are personnel issues – need more positions, have too many, etc.

? Are there any motivational issues mentioned?

? Were there ineffective concerns mentioned?

? What is the most important thing you learned today?

MATERIALS

✓ Cards on which questions are written – enough for each participant

✓ Chart tablet – optional

✓ Markers – optional

✓ Write pivotal questions dealing with current issues in the organization on cardstock. Possible questions might be:

- ❧ What is the status of our interaction with our customers?
- ❧ Is there a project that needs to be reviewed and possibly modified?
- ❧ How can we better serve our internal customers?
- ❧ What can be done to improve our market share?

....

The leader has to be practical and a realist, yet must talk the language of the visionary and the idealist. ~
ERIC HOFFER, AMERICAN MORAL AND SOCIAL PHILOSOPHER

....

SKILLSET	Starting the Journey		
TOOL	Bifocal Vision		
IMPACT	✓ Individual	✓ Team	✓ Group
PURPOSE	To project the major goals and concurrently see the "next steps"		

DESCRIPTION

- Group participants into teams. Each team is to identify one major future goal.

- Using bifocal eyeglasses as an analogy, select and write a goal at the top of the lens. Using this goal as the "farsighted" lens, have the participants then identify the "next steps" as the "nearsighted" lower part of the lens. Encourage the participants to be as thorough and detailed as possible.

- Have the team leader report the information to the group.

- Have the team prioritize the short-term steps for project completion.

DEBRIEF

? What are the major goals that need to be accomplished?

? What are the sequential steps needed to be done to accomplish the goals?

? How and to whom should these steps be assigned?

MATERIALS

✓ To illustrate the concept, provide a sketch of a pair of glasses on chart paper for each team

✓ Chart paper

✓ Markers

Farsighted Lens:
Goal

Nearsighted Lens:
Next Steps

· ·

Acting on a good idea is better than just having a good idea. ~ ROBERT HALF, AMERICAN HUMAN RESOURCE FIRM

· ·

SKILLSET	Starting the Journey		
TOOL	Family, Factory, Temple, and Jungle		
IMPACT	✓ Individual	✓ Team	✓ Group
PURPOSE	To assess a potential goal from different perspectives		

DESCRIPTION

- Candidly assess a potential goal, activity, project etc. through the following four perspectives (based on *Reframing Organizations*, Bowman & Deal, 1988, 2008). (See explanations provided.)

- Coach participants to look beyond the obvious and to consider the subtitles:

  - Human Resources: Family: Needs
  - Structural: Factory: Goals
  - Symbolic: Spiritual: Temple: Meaning
  - Political: Jungle: Power

- Using the chart (provided) list factors to be considered according to each perspective.

DEBRIEF

? What are the trends?

? What areas need to be addressed immediately?

? What actions can the leader take to move the organization to the next step?

? Will this effort (goal, activity, project, etc.) add value to the organization?

? If the issue is of value to the organization, what next steps will be required?

MATERIALS

✓ Chart

✓ Optional for large group processing: Chart tablet
    Markers

LEADERSHIP MODELS FOR REFRAMING ORGANIZATIONS

The Structural Framework

The "structural" leader tries to design and implement a process or structure appropriate to the problem and the circumstances. This includes:

clarifying organizational goals

managing the external environment

developing a clear structure appropriate to task and environment

clarifying lines of authority

focusing on task, facts, logic, not personality and emotions.

This approach is useful when goals and information are clear, when cause-effect relations are well understood, when technologies are strong and there is little conflict, low ambiguity, low uncertainty, and a stable legitimate authority.

The Human Resource Framework

The human resource leader views people as the heart of any organization and attempts to be responsive to needs and goals to gain commitment and loyalty. The emphasis is on support and empowerment. The HR manager listens well and communicates personal warmth and openness. This leader empowers people through participation and attempts to gain the resources people need to do a job well. HR managers confront when appropriate but try to do so in a supportive climate. This approach is appropriate when employee turnover is high or increasing or when employee morale is low or declining. In this approach, resources should be relatively abundant; there should be relatively low conflict and low diversity.

The Political Framework

The political leader understands the political reality of organizations and can deal with it. He or she understands how important interest groups are, each with a separate agenda. This leader understands conflict and limited resources. This leader recognizes major constituencies and develops ties to their leadership. Conflict is managed as this leader builds power bases and uses power carefully. The leader creates arenas for negotiating differences and coming up with reasonable compromises. This leader also works at articulating what different groups have in common and helps to identify external "enemies" for groups to fight together. This approach is appropriate where resources are scarce or declining, where there is goal and value conflict, and where diversity is high.

The Symbolic Framework

This leader views vision and inspiration as critical; people need something to believe in. People will give loyalty to an organization that has a unique identity and makes them feel that what they do is really important. Symbolism is important as is ceremony and ritual to communicate a sense of organizational mission. These leaders tend to be very visible and energetic and manage by walking around. Often these leaders rely heavily on organizational traditions and values as a base for building a common vision and culture that provides cohesiveness and meaning. This approach seems to work best when goals and information are unclear and ambiguous, where cause-effect relations are poorly understood and where there is high cultural diversity.

Retrieved from http://jenniferspates.blogspot.com/2008/02/leader-
  ship-models-fro-reframing.html

Goal/Activity/Project/etc.:	
Human Resource	Structural
Symbolic	Political

SKILLSET	Starting the Journey		
TOOL	Leadership in the Common		
IMPACT	Individual	✓ Team	✓ Group
PURPOSE	To identify behaviors of effective teams		

DESCRIPTION

- Give each participant or team a set of objects.

- Have the team members identify the uses of each object and infer implications for effective teamwork.

- Have a member of each team write the implications on chart paper.

- Have the teams report to the larger group.

DEBRIEF

? What can be learned from common objects and their usefulness?

MATERIALS

✓ Chart paper

✓ Markers

✓ Collection of objects: measuring cup, hammer, light bulb, packet of seeds, hinge, tire gauge, flower pot, wooden spoon, squish ball, straw, chocolate bar, artificial flower, etc.

Example: measuring cup — effective teams need to use measurement tools to chart progress

. . . .

Great leaders are almost always great simplifiers, who can cut through argument, debate, and doubt to offer a solution everybody can understand. ~ GENERAL COLIN POWELL, AMERICAN STATESMAN AND A RETIRED FOUR-STAR GENERAL IN THE UNITED STATES ARMY

. . . .

SKILLSET	Starting the Journey		
TOOL	The Ground Rules!		
IMPACT	Individual	✓ Team	✓ Group
PURPOSE	To establish a baseline of appropriate interactions in the team, department, etc.		

DESCRIPTION

- Engage the participants in a discussion on the need to have rules, laws, etc. Ask participants to think of meetings in which there were no expectations of behavior. Ask participants to suggest words that describe those meetings. Have a scribe record the words on a chart.

- Ask participants to suggest ground rules that would facilitate positive interactions in meetings and in ongoing office behavior. (If needed, suggest several possible ideas to get the group started. See below.) Have a scribe write the ideas as suggested.

- Once 10–15 possible ground rules have been identified, create an ad hoc team that will take the suggestions and refine the statements into 4–6 ground rules.

- Have the team bring the draft of the ground rules back to a subsequent meeting.

- Have one of the members of the ad hoc team present the refined list of ground rules to the total group. Ask for input for possible additional ideas or acceptance of the list.

DEBRIEF

? How can the rules be used and embedded into the normal activities of the organization.

? In practical terms, what do these rules look like?

MATERIALS

✓ Chart paper

✓ Markers

Sample A

Be constructive and supportive
Communicate openly
Respect others by listening with an open mind
Be open-minded and willing to participate
Be flexible, open to change
Be specific - use examples/research

Sample B

Listen when others speak
Be punctual
No labels
Be solution-oriented
Agree to disagree
Focus on the problem, not a personality

....

Every job is a self-portrait of the person who did it.
Autograph your work with excellence. ~ ANONYMOUS

....

SKILLSET	Starting the Journey		
TOOL	Map the Past, Project the Future		
IMPACT	Individual	✓ Team	✓ Group
PURPOSE	To honor past accomplishments and project next steps		

DESCRIPTION

- Identify three goals that were successful from the recent past.

- Assign one goal to each of three teams.

- Distribute a large sheet of chart paper and several colored markers to each team.

- Ask each team to draw a map depicting the steps required to achieve the goal that has been assigned to the team.

- Ask each team to recall challenges and opportunities encountered in pursuit of the goal and to use the road signs provided to pinpoint these challenges and opportunities on the map. (For example, challenges may be depicted by Road Closed, Dip, or Detour signs; opportunities by Scenic Route sign.)

- Suggest that the team use different color markers to indicate various steps in the process.

- Explain that the teams have 30 minutes to prepare their maps. (This timeframe can be flexible according to needs of the group.)

- Upon completion of the activity, post the maps on the wall.

- Have a member of each team explain the chart to the entire group.

DEBRIEF

? What challenges occurred that should be addressed in future work?

? What specific catalysts from the past assisted accomplishments?

? What lessons can be learned from the past to help us in achieving future goals?

MATERIALS/PRIOR PREPARATION
✓ Chart paper

✓ Markers

✓ Prepare a bulletin board or other large space for posting the maps

Possible Signs:

Choose those that are most appropriate for the organization.

....

"The future starts today, not tomorrow." ~ POPE JOHN PAUL II

....

SKILLSET	Starting the Journey		
TOOL	Progressive Knowledge		
IMPACT	Individual	✓ Team	✓ Group
PURPOSE	To identify the baseline of general understanding within the organization and to chart the progress throughout a given time period		

DESCRIPTION

- Identify a topic (goal, issue, etc.)

- Present the chart with K – W – L written at the top (provided). Explain the meaning of each letter:

  - K – Know – This is what we know about _____ (strategic plan, topic, etc.).
  - W – Want to know – These are the topics which need further research, information, etc.
  - L – Learned – As the quarter, year, given time period, progresses, the things that are learned are captured on the chart.

- Have the team process the K and W sections of the chart considering the topic. This can remain fluid so that as additional ideas arise, they can be added to the chart.

- Have one person maintain the chart as information is acquired. Express the necessity for such a chart to be in public view of the employees.

Note: This activity can be used at the start of and throughout a project.

DEBRIEF

? What are the areas that need specialized training?

? What are the specific ideas that need immediate attention?

? Are there other things that are dependent upon this?

? Should this information be prioritized?

? Under the "Want to Know," what are the priorities?

MATERIALS
- ✓ Chart paper with K – W – L chart drawn
- ✓ Markers

Topic:		
K – What we know	**W** – What we want to know	**L** – What we have learned

SKILLSET	Starting the Journey		
TOOL	Ripple Effect		
IMPACT	✓ Individual	✓ Team	✓ Group
PURPOSE	To assess a procedure/policy or examine a proposed plan of action		

DESCRIPTION

- Have participants work in teams of 2–4.

- Use the chart (provided) or draw the concentric circles on chart paper. Write the procedure, policy, or proposed plan of action in the innermost circle.

- Have participants brainstorm to identify the effect of the specified focus. Have the teams record the ideas generated in the appropriate circles.

- Have teams report to the whole group. Have a scribe capture the ideas on a large chart placed on a wall.

DEBRIEF

? Are there any noticeable trends?

? How can the organization use this information?

? Is there something needing to be changed in the organization which would impact the ripple effect?

? How can this information inform the goals of the organization?

MATERIALS

✓ Individual charts per participant or team (Note: Additional circles can be added per the dynamics of the organization.)

✓ Large paper for total group work

✓ Markers

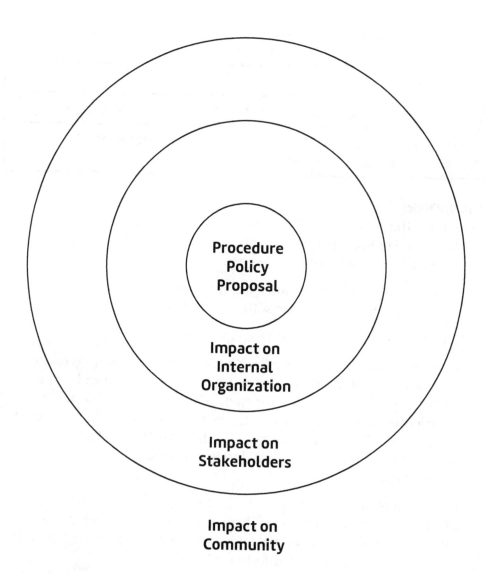

Procedure
Policy
Proposal

Impact on
Internal
Organization

Impact on
Stakeholders

Impact on
Community

ADAPTED FROM
Eller, S., & Eller, J. (2006). *Energizing staff meetings.* Thousand Oaks, CA:
Corwin Press.

···

*Be willing to make a decision. That's the most important
quality in a good leader. Don't fall victim to what I call
the "ready—aim—aim—aim—aim syndrome".*

~ T. BOONE PICKENS, AMERICAN MAGNATE AND FINANCIER

···

SKILLSET	Starting the Journey		
TOOL	Four Faces		
IMPACT	✓ Individual	✓ Team	✓ Group
PURPOSE	To identify the skills needed for a leader as he/she assumes a position		

DESCRIPTION

- Explain the concepts of risktaker, caretaker, surgeon, undertaker as delineated in Rothschild's, *Risktaker, Caretaker, Surgeon, Undertaker: The four faces of strategic leadership.*

- Have participants work in small groups, ideally about 3–5. This can also be done in a one-to-one setting or with a small leadership team.

- Give each team a copy of the chart (provided).

- Have them identify what practices, procedures, programs, etc. need to be started (risktaker), maintained (caretaker), revised with some parts removed (surgeon) and/or stopped (undertaker). (This will need to be a candid discussion due to the sensitive nature of the "personal ownership" of some of the activities. It is important that a thorough review of the organization be undertaken in order to assess the current status.)

- Have each team verbally report to the total group. (Caution the group that just because an activity has been mentioned and placed in a given category, it does not mean that action on it will occur immediately, if at all. This is an exercise to inform leadership.)

- Optional activity would be for a scribe to write the information as the teams are reporting.

DEBRIEF

? What are the themes that are emerging?

? Are there any red flags that appear?

? How does this inform the strategic planning for this organization?

? Are there any minefields that need to be avoided?

? Are there certain individuals that need to be involved for political or expertise reasons?

? On the major issues, what timeline should be established?

MATERIALS

✓ Charts

✓ Chart paper (optional)

✓ Markers

Risktaker (To begin)	Caretaker (To maintain)
Surgeon (To revise)	**Undertaker (To stop)**

SKILLSET	Starting the Journey		
TOOL	To Do, Doing, Done		
IMPACT	Individual	✓ Team	✓ Group
PURPOSE	To chart the progress of the specific tasks related to the major goals		

DESCRIPTION

- Have participants or teams responsible for different tasks related to meeting the major goals of the team or organization complete a card (provided) for each project. Separating the color of cards per team is visually helpful.

- Design a bulletin board or a large space on which cards can be posted and subsequently moved. Example provided.

- Have teams place their cards under the appropriate goal in the row labeled "To Do." As projects are begun, move the card to the next row (Doing). When the project is completed, the card is then moved to the bottom row (Done). (Note: There may be more than one card per team per goal – most likely so). Also, a given team may not have any cards under every goal.

- Periodically review the board to assess the status of the goal completion.

- As projects are completed, it is essential that some recognition be given. It is important that people see the progress.

DEBRIEF

? Are all goals sufficiently addressed by the different projects/activities?

? What can be done to ensure that all projects are completed to the level of expectation?

? How can everyone find his/her place of service in the bigger picture?

MATERIALS

✓ Cards – different colored cards per team/individual

✓ Bulletin board or similar space

Example of Cards:

Project _____

Goal Alignment _____

Description _____

Projected Start Date _____ Projected End Date _____

Team Member/Leader _____

Team Members _____

· ·

Goals not in writing are not goals at all. They are merely wishes or fantasies. ~ BRIAN TRACY, MOTIVATIONAL SPEAKER AND AUTHOR

· ·

Example of Bulletin Board:

	Goal 1	Goal 2	Goal 3
To Do			
Doing			
Done			

ANCHORS

As you begin the journey toward being an effective organizational leader, you must understand that your work will be scrutinized. It is essential for you to do your homework to be knowledgeable about the organization, the environment, and its people. You must know the desired outcomes, how to measure progress and use data for organizational improvement. Developing your relationships with co-workers and planning together are necessary.

Political figures have become accustomed to having their early days in powerful positions scrutinized and evaluated by the public. This has transferred into the business world. Books and plans such as *The First 90 Days* (Watkins, 2003) and *The New Leader's 100-Day Action Plan* (Bradt, Check, and Pedraza, 2006) have been popular guide books. Watkins (2003) warned that leaders are especially vulnerable in the first 90 days of their tenure because they lack a network of support and detailed knowledge of challenges to be faced.

> *Having a sense of purpose in your life is the most important element of becoming a fully functioning person.*
>
> ~ WILLIAM DYER, AMERICAN EDUCATOR

Albrecht (2003) suggested that many organizations are out of touch with their environment because they are preoccupied with internal matters and do not make time to keep in touch with their surroundings. He explained that environmental scanning provides a grounding in reality from which important learning can occur, such as identifying what competitors are doing. Environmental scanning serves as the foundation for strategic thinking.

In his work, *Start Where You Are*, Rouse (1996) stated that knowing where you are is key to getting where you want to go. He recommended that leaders assess current and future relationships within the marketplace:

First of all, like the captain of a sailboat, you are constantly attuned to your environment, what is happening in it, and what is likely to happen. Second, you understand the situations that are relevant in your environment and how you can recognize their emergence. Finally, of course, you understand your role in these situations and how you should respond. (p. 201)

Albrecht (2003) emphasized organizational scanning/digging below the surface to learn about the internal workings of the organization. Using the term 'historicizing', he suggested leaders ask six questions as a process for examining the history of a business to establish a perspective for considering its possibility for success in the future.

> What are we really good at?
> What do we reward, punish and condone?
> Are we a team?
> Do we learn and develop?
> Are we well led?
> Are we committed?" (pp. 80–103)

Continuing the emphasis on having knowledge of the internal organization, Ulrich, Smallwood, and Sweetman (2008) stated, "To be both visionary and analytic, strategic leaders must clearly understand their organization's current core competency, organizational capabilities, financial resources, and technology" (p 26). Parrott (2007a) asserted, "Committed leaders are expected to ensure the progress of the business by gathering and acting on the right information" (p. 101).

Become the kind of leader that people would follow voluntarily, even if you had no title or position.

~ BRIAN TRACY, MOTIVATIONAL SPEAKER AND AUTHOR

During organizational scanning, the importance of your knowing and assessing the people in the organization cannot be overstated. Sanborn (2006) declared that "Everything we accomplish happens not just because of our efforts but through the efforts of others. To accomplish any significant goal requires the support and cooperation of others...To get others to follow you requires character, competence, and connection..." (p. 53). Harvey, Cottrell, Lucia, and Hourigan (2003) emphasized that an organization's mission is accomplished primarily through employees. Therefore, hiring the right people is the most important responsibility of a leader.

Once environmental scanning and organizational scanning are underway, you must turn attention to strategies and tasks required to accomplish the organization's purpose. Nanus (1992), in *Visionary Leadership,* noted that "A vision is little more than an empty dream until it is widely shared and accepted" (p. 134). "Knowing where the organization should be headed is one thing. Developing a strategy for getting there is quite another" (p. 142). In the forward to *Visionary Leadership,* Bennis asserted that "Action without vision is stumbling in the dark; and vision without action is poverty-stricken poetry" (p. xv).

Considering the well-known adage, "Plan Your Work and Work Your Plan" in Volume 2 of his *Essential* series, Parrott (2007b) explained:

> *Without goals you have no stability... Goals give you desired power. The great thing... is not so much where we stand as in what direction we are moving.*
> ~ O.W. HOLMES, FORMER ASSOCIATE JUSTICE OF THE U.S. SUPREME COURT

> Writing a business plan for your organization is a skill you need to develop. First, learn to write a clear, workable plan that will organize your organization. A second skill you need is modeling the plan in your leadership responsibilities. The plan starts on paper, but must move into your daily habits, thoughts and action. There is a third skill in business planning. You must learn to share the plan with your staff. Your team must understand the plan and put it to work...A complete plan includes four parts.
>
> (1). Values and mission create the identity of the business.
>
> (2). Product/service centers describe what the business offers.
>
> (3) Goals/projects express what you expect to achieve.
>
> (4) The plan becomes actionable through your business model, a big picture of how you organize the staff. (pp. 50–52)

In *Navigating through Change,* Woodward (1994) recommended a three-step model for trying out and testing a plan:
1. Establish current reality — Establish an intellectual and emotional baseline.

2. Establish outcomes — Identify and clarify outcomes, solicit ideas, generate options for achieving outcomes, and what needs to be in place to achieve the outcomes.

3. Work backward. Move forward. — Test the plan, alter based on feedback.

Accomplishing the organizational purpose requires you to think strategically by establishing SMART goals, goals that are Specific, Measurable, Actionable, Realistic, and Timed. The FranklinCovey (2006) notebook, *Leadership: Great Leaders, Great Teams, Great Results*, explained the need for intentionally and openly tracking progress toward goals.

Great teams know at every moment if they are winning. A great score board is:

> Visible, located where everyone can see it;
>
> Visual, displays the lag and lead measures in one place;
>
> Engaging, attracts and holds attention;
>
> Doable, easy to administer;
>
> Concise, contains specifics such as from what to what and by when. (p. 69)

In the FranklinCovey notebook, Jim Stuart, senior consultant with FranklinCovey (2006) expressed that "People play differently when they are keeping score. When you create visible and dynamic scoreboards that display measures and progress, people know that they are playing 'for real'" (p. 69).

The need for keeping score was affirmed by Nanus (1992) who stated: "Monitoring involves gathering information about how well the vision is being implemented and measuring the organization's process in achieving the new direction" (p. 59). A process for this purpose, known as debriefing, was advised by Murphy (2005) in *Flawless Execution*. He asserted that, following planning and implementation, there must be intentional debriefing for the purpose of assessing progress toward goals. He suggested that debriefing is the most powerful tool by which companies can learn what has been done right or wrong. However, many organizations fail to debrief for two primary reasons: "First because time is money...Second, there is an understandable perception that rank and egos impede true debrief..." [However,] "debriefing is essential because it is how companies truly learn from their experience and react...almost in real time" (Murphy 2005, p. 134).

In summary, when embarking on the journey, you must engage in in-depth organizational planning. This requires:

- conducting environmental and organizational scans,

- establishing long-term objectives,

- breaking the objectives into short term goals and creating specific tasks,

- developing a process for obtaining feedback and a scoreboard for reporting, and

- periodically assessing and making strategic adjustments until objectives are achieved.

As you and your organization move toward accomplishing objectives, it is important that you establish a cyclical process of reflection to develop new goals.

. . . .

Your life will be no better than the plans you make and the action you take. You are the architect and builder of your own life, fortune, destiny. ~ ALFRED A. MONTAPERT, AMERICAN AUTHOR

. . . .

BEACONS – CITED REFERENCES

Examining Leadership

Bolman, L., & Deal, T. (2008). *Reframing organizations: Artistry, choice and leadership.* San Francisco: Jossey-Bass.

Collins, J. (2001). *Good to great: Why some companies make the leap...and others don't.* New York City: Harper Business.

Cottrell, S. (2010). *Skills for success: The personal development planning handbook.* New York City: Palgrave Macmillan Publishers, LLC.

Covey, S. R. (1989). *The 7 habits of highly effective people: Powerful lessons in personal change.* New York City: Free Press.

Covey, S. R. (2004). *The 8th habit: From effectiveness to greatness.* New York City: Free Press.

Drucker, P. (1974). *Management: Tasks, responsibilities, practices.* New York City: Harper & Row.

George, B. (2007). *True north: Discover your authentic leadership.* San Francisco: Jossey-Bass.

Green, H. (2012, September 25,). The top 5 leadership skills for sustained innovation. Retrieved from http://www.forbes.com/sites/work-in-progress/2012/09/25/the-top-5-leadership-skills-for-sustained-innovation/

Heider, J. (1985). *The Tao of leadership: Leadership strategies for a new age.* New York City: Bantam.

Jones, L. (1996). *The path.* New York City: Hyperion.

Kail, E. (2012, March 9). Leadership character: The role of reflection. Guest Insights Retrieved from http://www.washingtonpost.com/blogs/guest-insights/post/leadership-character-the-role-of- reflection/2011/04/04/glQAdJOr1R_blog.thml

Kouzes, J., & Posner, Z. (1997). Seven Lessons for Leading the Voyage to the Future in F. Hesselbein. et. al eds. *Anthology (The leader of the future: New visions, strategies and practices for the next era* (pp. 99-110). San Francisco: Jossey-Bass.

Leider, R. (1997). *The power of purpose.* New York City: Berrett-Koehler Publishers Inc.

Mutasak, L. (1997). *Finding your voice: Learning to lead anywhere you want to make a difference.* San Francisco: Jossey-Bass.

Parrott, R. (2006). *True & best: Authentic living.* Nashville: Seize Your Life, Inc.

Peel, B., & Peel, K. (1996). *Discover your destiny.* Colorado Springs: NAV Press.

Plato *(1656) Apology*, Jowett translation. Retrieved from
    http://www.gutenberg.org/etext/1656
Staropoli, F. (2000). *Reflection as a leadership fundamental*. Retrieved from
    http://www.staropoli.com/reflection.htm
Teatro, G. (2013). *Learned leadership by choosing to lead*. Retrieved February 26, 2013
    from http:gwynteatro

Charting Direction

Albrecht, K. (1994). *The northbound train: Finding the purpose, setting the direction,
    shaping the destiny of your organization*. New York City: AMACOM.
Barker, J. (Producer and Director) (1990). *The power of vision*. [Motion Picture]. United
    States: Star Thrower.
Barna, G. (1992). *The power of vision: Discover and apply God's vision for your life &
    ministry*. Ventura: Regal Books.
Bolman, L.,& Deal, T. (2008). *Reframing organizations: Artistry, choice, and leadership*.
    San Francisco: Jossey-Bass.
Covey, S.R. (1992). *Principled-centered leadership*. Houston: Free Press.
Covey, S.R. (2002). *Four roles of leadership*. Salt Lake City: FranklinCovey.
Covey, S. R. (2004). *The eighth habit: From effectiveness to greatness*. Houston:
    Free Press.
Heifezt, R. A. (1994). *Leadership without easy answers*. Cambridge, MA: Harvard
    University Press.
John F. Kennedy Presidential Library and Museum: Space Program. Retrieved from
    http://www.jfklibrary.org/JFK/JFK-in-History/Space-Program.aspx
Kearny, L. (1994). The facilitator's toolkit. Amherst, MA: HRD Press.
King, M.L. Jr. (1963). *I Have a Dream speech*. Retrieved from
    http://www.americanrhetoric.com/speeches/mlkihaveadream.html
Kouzes, J., & Posner, B. (2006). *A leader's legacy*. San Francisco: Jossey-Bass.
Kouzes, J., & Posner, B. (2007). *The leadership challenge*. New York: John Wiley & Sons.
Kouzes, J., & Posner, B. (2010). *The truth about leadership*. San Francisco: Jossey-Bass.
Parrott, R. (2007). *Essentials: The proven path of effective leadership*. Nashville: Seize
    Your Life, Inc.

Creating Authenticity

Bennis, W. (1989). *Why leaders can't lead*. San Francisco: Jossey-Bass.
Blanchard, K. (2010). *Leading at a higher level*. Upper Saddle River, NJ: Blanchard
    Management Corporation.
Covey, S.M.R. (2006). *The speed of trust*. New York City: Free Press.
Cox, D., & Hoover, J. (1992). *Leadership when the heat's on*. New York City: McGraw-Hill.
Fairholm, G. (2000). *Capturing the heart of leadership: Spirituality and community in the
    new American workplace*. Santa Barbara, CA: Praeger.
George, B. (2004). *Authentic leadership: Rediscovering the secrets to creating lasting
    value*. San Francisco: Jossey-Bass.
George, B., Sims, P., & Gergen, D. (2007). *True north: Discover your authentic leadership*.
    San Francisco: Jossey-Bass Publishers.
Hesselbein, F., & Goldsmith, M. (2006). *The leader of the future*. San Francisco:
    Jossey-Bass.

Hyatt, M. (2012, July 3). The five marks of authentic leadership. *Intentional Leadership.* Retrieved from http://michaelhyatt.com/the-five-marks-of-authentic-leadership.html

Irwin, T. (2009). *Derailed.* Nashville: Thomas Nelson.

Kouzes J., & Posner, B. (2006). *A leader's legacy.* San Francisco: Jossey-Bass.

Kouzes, J., & Posner, B. (2007). *The leadership challenge.* New York: John Wiley & Sons.

Kouzes, J., & Posner, B. (2010). *The truth about leadership.* San Francisco: Jossey-Bass.

Lennick, D., & Kiel, F. (2008). *Moral intelligence.* Philidelphia: Wharton School Publishing.

Lowney, C. (2003). *Heroic leadership.* Chicago: Loyola Press.

Merriam Webster Dictionary (2013) [electronic version]. Springfield, MA: Merriam Webster Inc.

Nayab, N. (2013, March 4). *Servant leadership vs. authentic leadership: What are the differences?* Retrieved from http://www.brighthub.com/office/home/articles/73574.aspx

Palmer, P. (2008). On the edge: Have the courage to lead with soul. *National Staff Development Chronicle, 29,* (2). Retrieved from: http://www.scsk12.org/scs/departments/professional-development/pdfs/lead-with-soul.pdf

Parrott, R. (2006). *True & best: Authentic living.* Nashville: Seize Your Life, Inc.

Senge, P. (1990, 2006). *The fifth discipline: The art and practice of the learning organization.* New York: Doubleday.

Shipka, B. (1997). *Leadership in a challenging world.* Newton, MA: Butterworth-Heinemann.

Spears, L. (Ed.). (1995). *Reflections on leadership.* New York City: John Wiley & Sons.

Delegating to Strengths

Baldoni, J. (2005). *Great motivation secrets of great leaders.* New York City: McGraw.

Bennis, W., & Townsend, R. (1995). *Reinventing leadership: Strategies to empower the organization.* New York City: William Morrow & Company, Inc.

Blanchard, K., & Hersey, P. (1988). *Management and organizational behavior.* Englewood Cliffs, NJ: Prentice Hall, Inc.

Business and Legal Reports, Inc. (2008). *Case study: The Ritz-Carlton mystique: Professionalism, high expectations.* Retrieved from http://www.talentplus.com/userfiles/pdf/The%20Ritz-Carlton%20Mystic.pdf

Covey, S.R. (2004). *The 8th habit: Reinventing leadership.* New York: Free Press.

Henman, L. (2010, September). *How to manage your employees' strengths.* Retrieved from http://www.executivetravelmagazine.com/articles/how-to-manage-your-employees-strengths

Parrott, R. (2007). *Essentials: The proven path of effective leadership.* Nashville: Seize Your Life, Inc.

Raelin, J. (2003). *Creating leaderful organizations.* San Francisco: Berrett-Koehler.

Reh, F. (2013). Delegate...don't just dump. *Management.* Retrieved from http:management.about.com/od/people/aDelegatDontDump.htm

Tough, M. (2004). *Delegate or die.* Retrieved from http://www.wisercafe.com/management/delegate-or-die

Aligning Operations

Albrecht, K. (1994). *The northbound train: Finding the purpose, setting the direction, shaping the destiny of your organization.* New York City: AMACOM.

Ashkenas, R.. Ulrich, D., Jick, T., & Kerr, S. (2002). *The boundaryless organization: Breaking the chains of organization structure.* San Francisco: Jossey-Bass.

Baldrige.com (2013, March 13). *Information you need to build the organization you want.* Retrieved from http://www.Baldrige.com/tag/deming

Bolman, L., & Deal, T. (2008). *Reframing organizations: Artistry, choice, and leadership.* San Francisco: Jossey-Bass.

Clemmer, J. (1993). *Firing on all cylinders.* Kitchener, ON: The Clemmer Group.

Covey, S.M., Covey, S.R., & Merrill, R. (2006). *The speed of trust: The one thing that changes everything.* Houston: Free Press.

Deming.org (2013, March 13). *The Deming system of profound knowledge.* Retrieved from http://deming.org/index.cfm?content=66

Hyatt, M. (2012, June 6). *How leaders can create alignment* [Podcast 015]. *Images for fishbone diagram.* (2013, March 13). Retrieved from https://www.google.com/search?q=fishbone+diagram&ie=UTF-8&oe=UTF-8&hl=en&client=safari

ORACLE. (2011a). *Employee excellence driving productivity and profit.* [Training PowerPoint]. Retrieved from http://www.oracle.com/oms/oracleday/oracle-hcm-solutions-jeddah-1445775.pdf

ORACLE. (2011b). *The importance and challenge of strategy alignment* [PowerPoint slide]. Retrieved from http://www.oracle.com/oms/oracleday/oracle-hcm-solutions-jeddah-1445775.pdf

Parrott, R. (2007). *Essentials: The proven path of effective leadership.* Nashville: Seize Your Life, Inc.

Senge, P. (2006). *The fifth discipline: The art and practice of the learning organization.* New York City: Doubleday Random House.

Stuart, J. (1999). *Four roles of leadership* [Facilitator's PowerPoint]. Salt Lake City, Utah: Franklin-Covey Company,

Starting the Journey

Albrecht, K. (2003). *The northbound train.* San Diego: Karl Albrecht International.

Bradt, G., Check, J., & Pedraza, J. (2006). *The new leader's 100-day action plan.* Hoboken, NJ: John Wiley & Sons, Inc.

FranklinCovey. (2006). *Leadership: Great leaders, great teams, great results.* Salt Lake City: FranklinCovey.

Harvey, E., Cottrell, D., Lucia, A., & Hourigan, M. (2003). *The leadership secrets of Santa Claus.* Dallas: The Walk the Talk Company.

Murphy, J. (2005). *Flawless execution.* New York City: Harper Collins Publishers.

Nanus, B. (1992). *Visionary leadership.* San Francisco: Jossey-Bass Publishers.

Parrott, R. (2007a). *Essentials: The proven path of effective leadership.* Nashville: Seize Your Life, Inc.

Parrott, R. (2007b). *Essentials: The proven path of effective leadership. Vol. 2: Planning and staffing.* Nashville: Seize Your Life, Inc.

Rothchild, W. (1993). *Risktaker, caretaker, surgeon, undertaker: The four faces of strategic leadership.* Holcomb, NJ: Wiley.

Rouse, W. (1996). *Start where you are.* San Francisco: Jossey-Bass Publishers.

Sanborn, M. (2006). *You don't need a title to be a leader.* New York: Doubleday Random House.

Ulrich, D., Smallwood, N., & Sweetman, K. (2008). *The leadership code: Five rules to lead by.* Boston: Harvard Business School Publishing.

Watkins, M. (2003). *The first 90 days.* Boston: Harvard Business School Press.

Woodward, H. (1994). *Navigating through change.* Burr Ridge, IL: Irwin Professional Publishing.

ADDITIONAL BEACONS

....

Examining Leadership

Bethel, S. (2008). *Making a difference: Twelve qualities that make you a leader.* Issaquah, WA: Made for Success Inc.

Block, P. (1993). *Stewardship: Choosing service over self-interest.* San Francisco: Berrett-Koehler Publishers.

Gilligan, S., & Dilts, R. (2009). *The hero's journey: A voyage of self discovery.* New York City: Crown House Publishers.

Guiliani, R. (2002). *Leadership.* New York City: Hyperion.

Kouzes, J., & Posner, Z. (2006). *A leader's legacy.* San Francisco: Jossey Bass.

Charting Direction

Barker, J. (1993). *Paradigms: The business of discovering the future.* New York City: Harper Business.

Bennis, W., & Nanus, B. (2007). *Leaders: The strategies for taking charge.* New York City: Harper Business.

Berry, T. (2000). *The great work: Our way into the future.* New York City: Broadway.

Bryson, J. (2011). *Strategic planning for public and nonprofit organizations: A guide to strengthening and sustaining organizational achievement.* San Francisco: Jossey-Bass.

Cockerell, L. (2008). *Creating magic: 10 Common sense leadership strategies from a life at Disney.* New York City: Crown.

Covey, S.M.R., Covey, S.R., & Merrill, R.R. (2006). *The speed of trust: The one thing that changes everything.* Houston: Free Press.

Covey, S.R. (1989). *The 7-habits of highly effective people: Powerful lessons in personal change.* Houston: Free Press.

Murphy, J. (2006). *Flawless execution: Use the techniques and systems of America's fighter pilots to perform at your peak and win the battles of the business world.* New York City: Harper Business.

Palmer, P. (2002). *The courage to teach: Exploring the inner landscape of a teacher's life.* San Francisco: Jossey-Bass.

Creating Authenticity

Baldoni, J. (2004). *Great motivation secrets of great leaders*. New York City: McGraw Hill.

Bennis, W., & Goldsmith, J. (2012). *Learning to lead*. Sydney, Australia: ReadHowYouWant.

Covey, S. R. (1992). *Principle-centered leadership*. Houston: Free Press.

Hunsaker, P. L., & Alessandra, A. J. (2008). *The art of managing people: Person-to-person skills, guidelines, and techniques every manager needs to guide, direct, and motivate the team*. New York City: Free Press.

Kouzes, J. M., & Posner, B. Z. (2011). *Credibility: How leaders gain and lose it...Why people demand it*. San Francisco: Jossey-Bass.

Delegating to Strengths

Buckingham, M., & Clifton, D. (2001). *Now, discover your strengths*. New York City: Free Press.

Blanchard, K., Carlos, J., & Randolph, A. (2001). *Empowerment takes more than a minute*. San Francisco: Berrett-Koehler.

Byham, W., & Cox, J. (1995). *HeroZ: Empower yourself, your coworkers, your company*. New York City: Ballentine.

Rath, T. (2009). *Strengths based leadership: Great leaders, teams, and why people follow*. Omaha: Gallup Press.

Zoglio, S. (1995). *The participative leader*. New York City: McGraw Hill.

Aligning Operations

Blanchard, K., & O'Connor, M. (1993). *Managing by values: How to put your values Into action for extraordinary results*. San Francisco: Berrett-Koehler.

Bossidy, L., & Charan, R. (2004). *Confronting reality: Doing what matters to get things right*. New York City: Crown Publishers.

Charan, R. (2007). *Know-how: The 8 skills that separate people who perform from those who don't*. New York City: Crown Publishers.

Covey, S. R. (1989). *The 7-habits of highly effective people: Powerful lessons in personal change*. Houston: Free Press.

Covey, S. R. (1992). *Principled-centered leadership*. Houston: Free Press.

Covey, S. R. (2002). *Four roles of leadership*. Salt Lake City: FranklinCovey.

Covey, S. R. (2004). *The eighth habit: From effectiveness to greatness*. Houston: Free Press.

King, M.L., Jr. (1963). *I Have a Dream* Speech. Retrieved from http://www.archives.gov/press/exhibits/dream-speech.pdf

Kouzes, J., & Posner, B. (2006). *A leader's legacy*. San Francisco: Jossey-Bass.

Kouzes, J., & Posner, B. (2007). *The leadership challenge*. New York: John Wiley & Sons.

Kouzes, J., & Posner, B. (2010). *The truth about leadership*. San Francisco: Jossey-Bass.

Murphy, J. (2006). *Flawless execution: Use the techniques and systems of America's fighter pilots to perform at your peak and win the battles of the business world*. New York City: Harper Business.

Palmer, P. (2002) *The courage to teach: Exploring the inner landscape of a teacher's life*. San Francisco: Jossey-Bass

Rothchild, W. (1993). *Risktaker, caretaker, surgeon, undertaker: The four faces of strategic leadership*. Holcomb, NJ: Wiley.

Starting the Journey

Buckingham, M., & Coffman, C. (1999). *First, break all the rules: What the world's greatest managers do differently.* New York City: Simon & Schuster.

Cloud, H. (2011). *Necessary endings: The employees, businesses, and relationships that all of us have to give up in order to move forward.* Boston: Harvard Business School Press.

Hickman, C., Smith, T., & Connors, R. (2010). *The Oz principle: Getting results through individual and organizational accountability.* New York City: Portfolio Trade.

Steiner, G. (1997). *Strategic planning.* New York City: Free Press.

Winston, S. (1996). *Stephanie Winston's best organizing tips: Quick, simple ways to get organized and get on with your life.* New York City: Touchstone.

KEEPERS OF THE LIGHT: CONTRIBUTORS OF TOOLS

In addition to the many individuals who have influenced the authors over the years, appreciation is extended to the following "Keepers of the Light" for their contributions to this volume. It is with gratitude that the names of contributors are listed below; at the same time it is with trepidation that some contributors may be overlooked. Others may not be named in that more than one submission of the same or similar activity has been received, or because of many years of use, the originator has been lost to memory.

Michelle Arnold
Sally Armstrong
Hazel Arthur
Allen Barger
Pam Bernards
Kristyn L. Boone
Daniel Brigman
Amelia Brock
David Bruce
Linda Cash
Wynona Constance
Laci Coppins
Delight Corbin
Dottie Critchlow
Sherry Dagnan
Coby Davis
Kelly Dodson
Callie Dollar
Jerry Doyle
Timothy Drinkwine
Russell Dyer
Allison Effinger

Deborah Fetch
Deborah Fields
Pamela Floyd
Ryan Forsythe
Vanessa Garcia
Renee Garriss
Sherry Gibbs
Melissa Gomez
Phillip Greeson
Marcia Harris
Terrance Haynes
Victoria Headrick
Regina Henry
Cheryl Horner
Jayson Huff
Steevon Hunter
Bobby Lee Hurley, Jr.
Susan P. Jones
Gregory Scott Kelley
Melissa Kennedy
Sarah King
Carol Malone

Anthony Manswell
Sharee Miller
Steven Moats
Dave Moore
Jeff Moore
Robbin Morthel
Robin Nichols
Adelaide Nicholson
Chris Nugent
Patty Poe
Sue Prather
Betty Roberts
Patti Robinson
Kristy Seccia
Eugene Terry
Martha Thweatt
Cassie Watson
Kim White
Cassie Wilkins
Tami Wilson
Margo Wimbish
Kathryn Woods

We continue to collect activities to enhance the skills of leaders who are endeavoring to build all aspects of their organizations. If you would like to contribute to the next volume, please give the reference of the activity or indicate that it is original to you. Submit an electronic copy to:

Esther Swink: eecs2014@yahoo.com
or
Ruth Cox : coxstrutzl@comcast.net

Any submission will be considered permission to publish.

We look forward to hearing from other "Keepers of the Light" and collecting more activities to assist leaders with tools for effective leadership.

Blessings and Godspeed,

Ruth Y. Cox, Ed. D.
Esther C. Swink, Ed. D.

ABOUT THE AUTHORS

The authors have 86 years of combined leadership experience in a variety of educational settings and levels. Both have worked as teachers, K-12 school administrators, professors and administrators at the undergraduate and graduate levels, and as consultants. Both are trained facilitators for FranklinCovey including *The 7-Habits of Highly Effective People.* Their philosophy is to actively engage learners in meaningful and practical ways. They founded RE-Lead to Re-Source emerging leaders with tools and activities for their journey, to Re-New the commitment of experienced leaders to organizational effectiveness, and to Re-Store organizational focus on values and goals, for the purpose of Re-Igniting commitment and passion.

Ruth Y. Cox is Professor of Education at Trevecca Nazarene University. She earned an Ed.D. in educational leadership from Nova University. She established and led an independent school, worked as a school and district level administrator in a large public school district, served as university professor and department administrator, held numerous organizational leadership positions, and actively worked as a community volunteer. She was nominated for the Eve Award.

Esther C. Swink is an independent educational consultant. She earned an Ed.D. in administrative leadership from Vanderbilt University. She directed school libraries and the work of several departments in a large public school system and served as professor and Dean of the School of Education in a private university. She has been an active volunteer and leader in numerous community organizations. She was nominated for the Athena Award.

CPSIA information can be obtained
at www.ICGtesting.com
Printed in the USA
LVHW112054240122
709248LV00007B/487